Frederick Whitfield, Charles W Quick

Counsels and Knowledge from the Words of Truth

Frederick Whitfield, Charles W Quick

Counsels and Knowledge from the Words of Truth

ISBN/EAN: 9783337248567

Printed in Europe, USA, Canada, Australia, Japan

Cover: Foto ©Thomas Meinert / pixelio.de

More available books at **www.hansebooks.com**

COUNSELS AND KNOWLEDGE

FROM

THE WORDS OF TRUTH.

BY
REV. FREDERICK WHITFIELD, M.A.,

SENIOR CURATE OF GREENWICH,
LATE INCUMBENT OF KIRBY-RAVENSWORTH, YORKSHIRE,
AND ASSISTANT MINISTER OF ST. GILES-IN-THE FIELDS, LONDON.

EDITED BY REV. CHARLES W. QUICK.

THIRD AMERICAN, FROM THE SECOND LONDON EDITION, REVISED.

PHILADELPHIA:
JAMES A. MOORE,
1220, 1222 AND 1224 SANSOM STREET.

INTRODUCTION

TO THE FIRST AMERICAN EDITION.

The distinguishing feature of the instructions of the author of this volume is his supreme exaltation of the word of God. The reader is not asked to compare his experience with previous frames and feelings, nor to measure himself by any human standard, however excellent and spiritual they may be. And further, he is neither required nor exhorted to adopt inspired patterns for his own guidance further than they are shewn by the Holy Spirit to have followed Christ. Such a feature and characteristic in these days of creature worship and of self-reliance cannot be too highly commended, and by those who prize the lively oracles of God those traits should be appreciated, and the works in which they appear conspicuously ought to be made available for doing good.

The reader of the following volume will find due honor given to the work of the Holy Spirit in calling, regenerating, and preparing covenant souls for "the inheritance of the saints in light." The entire dependence of the carnal and unregenerate sinner upon the sovereign and covenant work of the Third Person of the Trinity is brought out frequently, naturally, and without any strained effort.

"The wind bloweth where it listeth," but "the wind also goeth according to its circuits." In spiritual things the Spirit moves or rests, is strong or gentle; it whispers in the still small voice of sadness and seriousness, or roars in the conscience with the loud storms of deep and pungent conviction, all as He pleaseth, "dividing to every one severally as He will." "For, thus saith the Lord, as the rain cometh down, and the snow from heaven, and returneth not thither, but watereth the earth, and maketh it bring forth and bud, that it may give seed to the sower, and bread to the eater: so shall my word be that goeth forth out of my mouth: it shall not return unto me void, but shall accomplish that which I please, and it shall prosper in the thing whereto I sent it. Isaiah lv, 10, 11.

The careful and experienced author also brings out the revealed fact that the Holy Spirit uses the word of God written, and the testimony of Jesus as therein contained, for the chief and God-glorifying means of all his operations. He may be pleased to work *immediately* upon some minds, but whenever means are used, the word of God is exclusively used. The public or private teacher can have no warrant for any other means, and no hope for success in the use of any other truth than that which is in Jesus and presented as it is in Jesus.

The reader will not find a systematic arrangement of Bible truth, nor any connected series of expository discourses. The familiar expositions of different portions of Scripture are reproduced as they were given, and arising out of the varied occurrences of a pastoral and parochial connection. They show that the mind of the under shepherd was carefully watching the dealings of Providence connected with the people of his charge, and, as far as possible, the progress of the Spirit's work in their ever changing and fresh Christian experience, or in the want of such experience. And, according to his discernment, the faithful watchman divided to each a portion of the word of truth. This accounts for the familiar, personal, and affectionate style of writing. The flow of thought, and the tone of earnestness show a deep personal interest and anxiety for the welfare of the people instructed, which cannot be supposed applicable to others remote from his field of labor. But in proportion as any one making use of the volume for public instruction and effort has a burden of interest in the soul's welfare of those providentially brought in contact with him, in the same degree he will enter with entire sympathy into the fervid spirit, the tender persuasiveness, and the solemn engagedness of the gifted author.

We feel convinced that the promoter and prompter of that earnestness which characterizes the writings and preaching of the author will not escape the notice of the reader, as we trust it will not fail to charm and influence him. It is stated in the preface, and felt all through his works, and is the hope of the waiting Church, "the glorious appearing of our Great God and Saviour, Jesus Christ." [Gr. T.] This hope was the strong anchor and the strong consolation of the Apostles and of their immediate converts. For ages it remained the great comfort of the persecuted and tried household of the faith, and in late years it has been revived and is now hailed and cherished by an increasingly large proportion of those who enjoy "the common salvation." There is "one hope of our calling," and that is the hope, not of the individual, but of the body of Christ as such. It is not varied by frames and feelings, and according to its brightness will be the believer's deadness to the world and his conformity unto the image of the Son of God.

In the making up of the present volume it was found that several pages were needed to complete the last form, and these have been filled with matter of the same general kind, and, as far as possible, imbued with the same evangelical spirit. And now, with the sole desire of promoting the Gospel, and of enlarging the extent and influence of a testimony for Christ of peculiar directness and clearness, this box of spikenard is presented to the readers to whom God in His providence may, through the efforts of the Lord's people, send it. To them we would say in the words of the Apostle Paul, "Therefore, my beloved brethren, be ye steadfast, unmoveable, always abounding in the work of the Lord, forasmuch as ye know that your labor is not in vain in the Lord." 1 Cor. xv, 58.

C. W. Q.

JULY, 1873.

PREFACE.

"Have not I written to thee excellent things in *counsels and knowledge,* that I might make thee know the certainty of *the words of truth;* that thou mightest answer the words of truth to them that send unto thee?" (Prov. xxii, 20, 21). I trust that my book may in some small measure fulfill this, the great design at all times of the Holy Spirit, in making known the truth as it is in Jesus.

At the request of several correspondents, I have purposely made the chapters of this book shorter than those of my previous volumes, in order that they may form family readings for Sunday or week-day; the chapters in the previous works being too long for this purpose.

They have been written in the intervals of pressing duties, and form the *outlines,* many of them, of sermons preached in the parish church of Tunbridge, while it was my privilege to be there as its temporary minister. I trust, though there is little about them worthy of meeting the public eye, there may be some few grains of truth in the midst of the chaff by which they are surrounded, which the God of all grace may use for His glory.

How solemn and startling are the times in which we live! Whether we look at them nationally, politically, socially, or religiously, clouds are gathering over our horizon, of a deep and dark hue, and with which no previous history of our world furnishes a parallel. The tragical character of the murders which of late years have stained the columns of our press, the startling revelations of trades-unionism, the atrocities of Fenianism, the increasing worthless account in which human life is held, all are lines in the dark picture, of a unique character. If we look at the Church, we see a picture equally saddening. Romanism, Rationalism, and Ritualism are advancing with giant strides. Mark the fierceness of the contending parties, as the thick of the battle is approaching, threatening to culminate in deadly feuds. If we look at the general aspect of Europe, at those kingdoms over which imperial Rome once bore sway, what do we see? Under the appearance and profession of friendship, there is a universal preparation for war by increasing their respective armaments. If we look at things *generally*, is it not true that with regard to everything, both of good and evil, the lines of things are becoming more distinctly marked? The *reserve* of past years is giving way to *definite utterances*. Each year, as it rolls over our heads, seems to give a coloring to the outline, to intensify the picture. And though it is true that as each wave beats upon the shore of time, and the echoes of it still linger on our ears, we are apt to regard it as more important than that of any previous year, simply because the lines of the previous ones have faded from the memory, yet notwithstanding all this, does not each one as it comes round assume an importance possessed by no previous one? Is it not pregnant with more startling events, and with a deeper meaning? Where will all this end? What shall be the issue? The child of God is at no loss for an answer. They are hastening on the goal of his wishes. The night grows darker, but it only shrouds an unsetting sun. The day-dawn shall soon arise. With all the constellations of the universe encircling His brow, the clouds so big with judgment shall shortly disclose to our enraptured view the King of kings and Lord of lords.

But in the meantime the night is growing darker, and many a weary and foot-sore traveler to Zion is out on the open plain. As the deepening shadows fall around, they bid him gird his garments about him and hasten his footsteps. They warn him to tarry not in all the plain, to look not behind him, but to press onward with renewed energy to the city of light that gleams in the distance. The faint echoes of the trumpet cry are falling on his ears from that city, "Behold, the Bridegroom cometh." Burnish the rusted armor! Brighten the waning lamp! Gird up the trailing garments! Grasp the sword of the Spirit firmly in hand! The foe is at the door! Woe to him who is found slumbering on the field! "Rise, and let us go hence." Watch and pray. Clear the hands of every inconsistency. Let no cloud or shadow hinder the light of a Saviour's countenance falling on the soul. Have done with compromise and concession. Be whole-hearted for Christ. Whatever you neglect, beware of neglecting secret communion with God. Whatever it may cost you, see that you are found clearly and unmistakably on the Lord's side. If you would have Him faithful to you in an hour which will be of all others most trying, see that you are His now —wholly His, clearly His, and none but His.

Reader, may the Lord find you so when He shall come!

BOZEAT VICARAGE,
    WELLINGBOROUGH,
        March, 1868.

CONTENTS.

	PAGE
GRACE ABOUNDING	11
LIVING SACRIFICES	21
PAUL'S ADDRESS AT ANTIOCH	29
THE PASSAGE OF THE JORDAN	43
THE SYRIAN LEPER	53
THE ASCENDED SAVIOUR	66
ISRAEL IN THE WILDERNESS	81
THE GOOD PROFESSION	88
THE SUPPER CHAMBER	97
THIRSTING FOR GOD	102
GOD'S ANSWER TO THE SINNER'S QUESTION	110
THE WOMEN AT THE SEPULCHER	118
THE BLIND MAN OF BETHSAIDA	125
LESSONS FROM THE WELL OF SYCHAR	133
BREAD CAST ON THE WATERS	148
CONTRASTS	159
SIMEON IN THE TEMPLE	168
PARTING WORDS	183
THE COMING OF CHRIST	194
THE COMMUNION OF SAINTS	203

COUNSELS AND KNOWLEDGE FROM THE WORDS OF TRUTH.

GRACE ABOUNDING.

Psalm cv, 39—43.

"He spread a cloud for a covering, and fire to give light in the night. *The people* asked, and he brought quails, and satisfied them with the bread of heaven. He opened the rock, and the waters gushed out; they ran in the dry places *like* a river. For he remembered his holy promise, *and* Abraham his servant. And he brought forth his people with joy, *and* his chosen with gladness."

The history of Israel in the desert is but the counterpart of the history of the Church of the living God in her passage through this world. It is a history of God's grace triumphing over man's sin. On the one hand, we behold murmuring, rebellion, unbelief, and sin; on the other, long-suffering, forbearance, wondrous grace, and unchanging love. Such are the striking features in the portion of Scripture we have selected for consideration.

How graciously the Spirit of God in these verses throws a veil over the failings and sins of Israel! The people ask, but nothing is said of the sin connected with their asking. The people have the rock opened for them, but their unbelief connected with that opening is passed over. True, this part of their history has its place, but not here. The Spirit of God is, throughout this chapter, bringing to view all the sins and iniquities of their *enemies*. When His own people are placed alongside of them, He seems to say, "I have not beheld iniquity in Jacob." When, however, He deals with them apart from their enemies, in the next chapter, when they are alone in the desert, then all their sins and failings are drawn with the point of a diamond, and the needed discipline to correct it. *Before their foes,* Israel is all perfection, and God all grace. *Alone in the desert,* He causes them to pass under the rod to purge away their dross. Thus is God at all times. To the *world* He says, "He that toucheth one of these little ones, it were better for him that a millstone were hanged about his neck, and he cast into the sea." To *them* He says, "You only have I known of all the families of the earth: therefore will I punish you for your iniquities."

"He spread a cloud for a covering: and fire to give light in the night." This cloud was the vehicle of the Divine presence (see Exodus xiv, 19–24). It is referred to again in Isaiah vi, 4. It is the cloud of glory alluded to so frequently in Ezekiel's vision. It is the same as that on the mount of transfiguration, and on the mount of ascension. The Lord Jesus is seen in the cloud. He is the true "covering" of His people. He it is that is "spread" over them by day and by night during their wilderness journey. He is their "light" in the night. He "goeth before them," calling them by name, and leading them in and out of the fold that they may find pasture. He is their "covering" from every charge of sin, in every hour of sorrow, in every moment of danger. Whatever foe might advance to assail Israel, it had to meet the cloud, and the arrow that would reach the feeblest of Israel's ranks must first go through it. The Shepherd "goeth before" His sheep, not only as their Leader, but first to encounter the foe, and to remove every obstacle in their way. Such was the God-spread covering of Israel. Such is Christ, the true covering spread by Heaven over every child of the kingdom.

Not only so, it was theirs *forever*. Whatever else might be taken away, that would never be removed (see Exodus xiii, 22). They fell into sin, but the cloud was there. They murmured, rebelled, wandered from God; still the cloud left them not. So it is with Jesus. Peter fell; the sons of Zebedee fell; all the disciples forsook Him and fled: *their* history, like Israel's of former days, and like ours in this day, was one of constant failure and sin. Yet He never left them. When all others failed He was true. And God's continued word to His people, whether in Old or New Testament history, is, " Fear not: for I am with thee;" " Lo, I am with you always." " He took not away the pillar of the cloud by day, nor the pillar of fire by night from before the people." " Having loved His own which were in the world, He loved them to the end." " I will never leave thee, nor forsake thee." " I have *graven* thee on the palms of my hands; thy walls are *continually* before me." " Why sayest thou, O Jacob, and speakest, O Israel, My way is hid from the Lord, and my judgment is passed over from my God? Hast thou not known? hast thou not heard, that the everlasting God, the Lord, the Creator of the ends of the earth, fainteth not, neither is weary? there is no searching of His understanding. He giveth power to the faint; and to them that have no might He increaseth strength. Even the youths shall faint and be weary, and the young men shall utterly fall: but they that wait upon the Lord shall renew their strength; they shall mount up with wings as eagles; they shall run, and not be weary; and they shall walk, and not faint."

The "cloud" was indeed a "covering." It was the most perfect expression of the Lord Jesus on record. It went with Israel from the very midst of Egypt to the very borders of Canaan—that is, from the very moment it was needed, till it was needed no longer. It was in the wilderness, because Israel was there. It was just whatever Israel needed it to be. No man dwelt where Israel was about to travel. There were no sign-posts there, no bread, no water. It led them to the rock and brought food to feed them. It made them independent of highways and sign-posts in the trackless wilderness. If they needed cloud and fire, it was that. If they needed light and darkness, it was that; and this at the self-same moment. It is destruction and death if they need that; for the glory of Egypt withers under the Eye that looks through it, and the host is troubled and overthrown. And is not Jesus all this now to His people? Mark the moving of this holy cloud in the New Testament! See if He was not then all this and much more to His people! And such is He still to each one, the weakest and feeblest in the camp. "I am the Lord, I change not; *therefore* ye sons of Jacob are not consumed."

"The people asked, and He brought quails, and satisfied them with the bread of heaven." A veil is thrown over the sin connected with their asking. God meets us according to the riches of His grace, and not according to our deserts. They ask, and the quails, or small red partridges, come and surround the camp. He satisfies them with the bread of heaven. Christ is the living bread which came down from heaven. If the soul of man is indeed to be *satisfied*, it must be by something *above this world*. Over every stream of joy on earth there is written with the pen of heaven, "Whosoever drinketh of this water shall thirst again." Only Jesus can *fill* man's craving void. The world may tempt and dazzle and excite; but man, to be *satisfied*, must look elsewhere. The eye on Jesus, there is satisfaction. The heart filled with Jesus, there is joy. The burden laid on Jesus, oh, there is rest! Reader, do you know it? Do you know it by *experience?* You can never enter into joy till joy enters into you. The only joy which is not mockery is, to know Jesus. To know Him is to have passed from death unto life. That soul has eternal life *now*, and only waits for the resurrection *body*. The new *life* must have a new *body* to match it. The *one* we have in knowing Jesus; the *other* we shall have very shortly.

"He opened the rock, and the waters gushed out." In 1 Corinthians x, 4, we are told that "that Rock was Christ." By referring to the Books of Exodus and Numbers we see how that rock was opened. The first command to Moses was to "*smite* the rock." On the second occasion he was told to "*speak* to the rock." Moses, however, in rashness and unbelief disobeyed God, and instead of *speaking* to the rock, he *smote* it again. For this he was visited with judgment. The application of this truth is most instructive. Christ is the Rock. He was once *smitten;* and on the cross of Calvary the living streams to cleanse the soul of the sinner issued forth. But having been *once* smitten, He needs not to be smitten again. "By *one* offering He hath perfected forever them that are sanctified." We need no *repeated* sacrifice. We have now only to "*speak* to the Rock." Nay, to attempt a repetition is to show our unbelief in the efficacy of that perfect sacrifice. To *smite* the Rock again, is simply to say we do not believe in the *finished* work of the Lord Jesus. The Rock *has been* smitten; the blood *has been* shed; the work is "finished." Now, the command is, *Speak* to the Rock." This is all that is needed to bring down the healing streams—" the living waters from the river of life." The moment the soul that has looked to Jesus and found peace begins to doubt, he *smites* the Rock again—he doubts the efficacy of the atoning blood. No, no. The work is *done*. Sin is *gone*. God sees none on your soul. Hear His cry to thee, trembling one, from the cross, "It is finished." Thy pardon is sealed. Thy salvation is finished, even *thine*. Smite not that Rock again. *Speak* to the Rock, speak in confidence, speak in thankfulness, speak in praises, speak, and plead the smitten virtues of the one offering once offered for thy sins. Art thou burdened? speak to the Rock. Art thou wounded? speak to the Rock. Art thou forsaken and alone? speak to the Rock. Do troubles assail? do looks change? do smiles vanish? speak to the Rock. Does disease invade the trembling house of clay? are the pillars of thy heart's shrine crumbling beneath thee? does the cold river of death spread itself before thy view? speak to the Rock. At all times, in all places, for all purposes, in the battle of life or in the stillness of the dying chamber, "speak to the Rock," "speak to the Rock."

"*He* opened the rock." Not *thy* prayers, but God's grace. Not *thy* speaking, but His deep compassion. Not because of anything in *thee*, but because He has set His love upon thee. Oh, yes! Remember it always, "*He opened the rock.*"

"And the waters *gushed* out." What a sweet expressive word, they "*gushed*" out! See the illustration! A compassionate loving being visits the abodes of wretchedness in one of our large towns. Suddenly a haggard, shattered wreck of our fallen humanity is presented to her notice. For a moment she gazes; then the bosom heaves, and the pent-up heart gives way to a flood of tears. This is the gushing of the heart at the sight of misery. Pent-up compassion is drawn out in a flood-tide of love. Such was the Rock. It was full to overflowing. It needed but the word to disclose its refreshing streams, so that the waters ran in the dry places like a river. Such was Christ. Oh the deep compassions that were pent-up in the bosom of that humble Man! Mark two or three instances in which the waters gushed out from this smitten Rock, and ran in the dry places of our world like a river. "And there came a leper to Him, beseeching Him, and kneeling down to Him, and saying unto Him, If Thou wilt, Thou canst make me clean. And Jesus, *moved with compassion*, put forth His hand and touched him, saying, I will; be thou clean." Mark another. "And Jesus, when He came out, saw much people, and was *moved with compassion* toward them, because they were as sheep not having a shepherd, and He began to teach them many things." Again: "When He beheld the city, He *wept* over it, saying, If thou hadst known, even in this thy day, the things that belong to thy peace: but now they are hid from thine eyes." Oh how the living waters *gushed* out from this Rock, and filled the dry places of many a poor wanderer's heart in the highways of Galilee and Judæa! There was no short measure, no half-opened hand, no mental reservation. No; grace came forth from the bosom of infinite Love in an overflowing stream. Wherever He went, men "*spake to the Rock;*" spake by their sins, their sorrows, their needs; and "the waters ran in the dry places like a river." One who had experienced the grace of that Rock more deeply than most, exclaims, "My God shall supply *all your need,* according to His riches in glory in Christ Jesus." Sinner, see what a precious Saviour is thine! See, poor trembling one, the gushing tide of love in that bosom! Measure it not by thy thoughts; it infinitely exceeds them all. Judge not of *that* heart by *any* picture, even the most exalted. No thought can conceive its fullness, no line can sound its depth. "The well is deep," deeper far than all the needs of thy needy soul. Say not, "Can He love *me?*" Say not, "I fear *I* am too bad." Say not, "Will He receive *me?*" Behold the gushing tide of love in that bosom ready to roll "like a river" over all thy sin and guilt and misery! Behold it all *thine!* Grieve that love no longer by such sinful doubts. Cast no dishonor on that precious Saviour's name. "*Speak* to the Rock;" speak *now* in faith, in thankfulness and praise— "*My* Lord and *my* God!"

Child of God, are there no dry places in thy soul? are there none around thee? "Yea," thou art ready to exclaim, "My soul thirsteth for Thee, my flesh longeth for Thee, in a dry and thirsty land where no water is." Oh then, "*speak* to the Rock," "*speak* to the Rock." Let nothing come between thy soul and God. Let no carelessness of walk, no inconsistency of conduct, no compromise with what is grievous to God's Spirit, dim thine eye, or draw a cloud between thy soul and Jesus. "*Speak* to the Rock," speak often. Let nothing rob thy soul of secret fellowship with Jesus. Let no earthly claim, however important, allow thee to cut short the time devoted to this end. Live in His presence. Let the light of His countenance shine clearly on thy soul. Be found, "*in* season and *out* of season," near the Rock. Then will all go well with thy soul.

s Jesus the covering of His people? Is He their light in the night? Does He satisfy them with the bread of heaven? Does He open the rock that the waters gush out? Then remember the source of it all, "for He remembered His holy promise and Abraham His servant." Remember, they all proceed from the covenant recorded in the fifteenth chapter of Genesis. Those divided pieces were a type of the smitten Lamb of God. In blessing Israel with all these blessings, it was because He remembered that covenant. *It* was before God's eye continually. *Love* makes memory retentive. God beholds and remembers the sacrifice of His dear Son on Calvary. *It* is very precious to Him. He *so* loved Him that memory ever brings before Him that sacrifice. For the sake of that sacrifice we are blessed. For the sake of that sacrifice "joy and gladness" are the heritage of His people, and the smile of heaven falls unceasingly upon us. Let us not forget the little word with which this passage opens, "for He *remembered* His holy promise and *Abraham* His servant. And He brought forth His people with joy and His chosen with gladness."

Precious Saviour! what a treasure art Thou to Thy people! O sinner, taste and see how gracious He is!

" But *what* to those who find?
Ah this no tongue can utter; this
No mortal tongue can show.
The love of Jesus, what it is,
None but His loved ones know."

Blessed be God, our God!
Who gave for us His well-beloved Son,
The Gift of gifts, all other gifts in one.
Blessed be God, our God!

What will He not bestow,
Who freely gave this mighty Gift, unbought,
Unmerited, unheeded, and unsought,
What will He not bestow?

He spared not His Son!
'Tis this that silences each rising fear;
'Tis this that bids the hard thought disappear;
He spared not His Son!

Who shall condemn us now,
Since Christ has died, and risen, and gone above,
For us to plead at the right hand of Love?
Who shall condemn us now?

'Tis God that justifies.
Who shall recall His pardon or His grace?
Or who the broken chain of guilt replace?
'Tis God that justifies!

The victory is ours!
For us in might came forth the mighty One;
For us He fought the fight, the triumph won;
The victory is ours!

BONAR.

LIVING SACRIFICES.

Romans xii, 1, 2.

"I beseech you therefore, brethren, by the mercies of God, that ye present your bodies a living sacrifice, holy, acceptable unto God, *which is* your reasonable service. And be not conformed unto this world: but be ye transformed by the renewing of your mind, that ye may prove what *is* that good, and acceptable, and perfect will of God."

THE word "therefore" occurs very frequently in the New Testament as we open the chapter. It is the golden link which connects the chapter with that which has preceded it. We shall always do well to look back and see this connection before we proceed. It is a word that in *every case* throws light on what is to follow. Mark it in these opening verses. In the previous chapter (verses 27, 30—32) the apostle had been speaking of God's mercy to Jews and Gentiles, by the putting away of sin. The word "therefore" in the opening words of this portion of Scripture connects the "mercies of God" with the passages referred to. The basis of entreaty to holiness are these "mercies of God." All exhortation to holiness of life must have a motive from which that holiness is to spring. To exhort a man to give up sin and to be holy, without that man having a motive for it, is simply impossible. Man loves sin, and cannot give it up. It is his *nature* to love it. But let the Spirit of God only show him his sin, and the love of God in having forgiven that sin, then he has a powerful lever within for throwing off sin. "The love of Christ constraineth" him. Now this is what is set before us here. Men are "*besought*" to be holy "*by the mercies of God.*" All attempts at holiness without this are only so many self-righteous efforts. Do not ask men to give up sin, give up the race-course, the ball, the dance, the concert. They cannot do it. They *love* the world, and to it they will go. It is the very height of folly to preach in this way. But let the "love of the Father" enter; let them see Jesus; then such exhortations may be, *ought* to be, addressed. Men love these things because "the love of the Father is not in them." Let that enter in, and they cannot "love the world." Their language will be that of Ephraim of old, "What have I to do any more with idols?"

But what is it believers are to "present"? Their "bodies." We should have expected to hear the apostle say "your *souls.*" But no, it is the *body.* Why is this? Because *it* is the avenue through which all sin enters the soul. The eyes, the ears, the tongue, the hands, the feet; these are some of the avenues to the soul by which sin enters. And therefore the Spirit of God begins with the body, the broad road by which all travelers enter the citadel. These members of the body, both individually and corporately, the believer is to "present." The word is an allusion to the "presenting" of the sacrifices by the priest on the altar. Each part of the slain lamb was to be presented, piece by piece, in due order. So the believer is now a "priest unto God." Like the priest of old, he stands in the very presence of God. He is never out of it. Like the priest of old, too, each *member* of the sacrifice is to be laid on the altar, Christ Jesus, to His glory. His eyes, his ears, his hands, his feet, are to be laid out, hour after hour, to God's glory. Not indeed now, like the sacrifices of old, having the blood, the life, *poured out*, but having the life *in*. But what life? The new life; the life of Christ. That life is now in the soul, because Christ Himself is there. "Know ye not that your bodies are the temples of the Holy Ghost?" Therefore it is that the sacrifices are "*living* sacrifices." Only this can make any believer be a "*living*" man. Christ is in him, "the hope of glory." Therefore all is *life*, real life, everlasting life. Therefore the whole man in all his parts is to be presented as a "sacrifice, holy, acceptable to God." It is a "*reasonable* service." God is not unreasonable. He asks not more than we by His Spirit's power can give. Has He indeed *shown* such mercy to us while sinners? Has He multiplied His mercies every day and every hour? Then indeed it is only "reasonable" that we should lay out all to His glory. It is the service of an intelligent creature. He has bought us. We are not our own. Therefore we are to glorify God in our bodies, and in our spirits, which are the Lord's."

We may notice two aspects in these verses. In the first, the believer is brought before us in relation to God. In the second, he is viewed in relation to the world in which he lives. He is to "present his body a living sacrifice" to God. But then he is in the "world," and that world is the great hindrance to this. On every side and in every hour of the day, influences are playing upon him counteracting God's work. This is the dazzling, blinding, ensnaring world, under the government of "the prince of the power of the air, the spirit that now worketh in the children of disobedience." In this world lies all his danger. There are two moulds; one is the Spirit of God, the other is the world. The Christian is like the molten metal. Into which of these moulds will he be cast? He may be a Christian, and yet so walk as to be moulded by "this present world." Do we not see Christians on every side with the marks and shadows of the world written but too plainly on them? Do we not see one who shows only too clearly that he has fallen into the world's mould, and *it* has shaped him? Surely the sad picture is on every side of us. Here then is the danger. He is a Christian in the *world*, and that is a *terrible* thing! He is in a place of continued and imminent danger. By which will he be moulded? The command is, "Be not conformed," or *moulded*, into its likeness; not only so, but "be ye transformed;" that is to say, be *the very opposite*. If the world goes one way, do you go the opposite. There is to be no compromise, no extenuation, no meeting it half way, no saying, like Lot, of old, "Is it not a little one?" No; "be ye *transformed*." Say to *it*, as Abram said to Lot, "If thou go to the right hand, I will go to the left; and if thou go to the left, I will go to the right."

Then how is this moulding of the Christian into the very opposite shape of the world to be carried out? The apostle tells us; "by the *renewing* of your *mind*." Here, again, he would seem to take us back to the temple. No doubt it was before his mind. We know that in that service it was the duty of the priest, morning and evening, to renew the lights of the tabernacle by pouring the oil into the vessels. As the light became dimmer and dimmer, its brilliancy was "renewed" by replenishing the vessel with oil. The believer is that vessel, the light shining in the dark place. But that light must be daily renewed or it will burn dimly. The Holy Spirit must be poured day by day into that vessel in large measure. He must take of Christ and daily show Him to the soul. He must work in that vessel, bringing his thoughts and affections, his desires and hopes, his words and ways, into subjection to the word of God. He must show him more and more of his own heart, more of his helplessness and emptiness, and make him cling more closely than ever to Jesus. Thus the vessel will be replenished. Thus the light will shine. Thus the man will be transformed, cast into the very opposite mould of the world. Thus will he be shaped and moulded into the likeness of the Son of God. Thus, but, reader, lay it well to heart, *only thus*.

But mark one caution. This transformity to the world must not be according to some standard of our own. It must not be transformity according to some fancy of ours as to what this worldliness is. How sad are the mistakes on this point! How often have we heard of rank renouncing its title; of one in a high position of life renouncing voluntarily that position, and coming down to the lowest level of society, instead of using it for God! How often have we seen the neat apparel renounced for slovenliness of dress? how often the well furnished house for bare boards and plain fare? How often has all this been the case, with the secret, undetected self flattery that *we* have done something for God; that *we* have come to that spiritual standing and position superior to other Christians around us! How often with the spirit of renunciation has another spirit crept in and gradually gained ascendancy, so as to leave the soul in a far worse state than before. Ah! let us beware of this kind of transformity. True transformity to the world is to *stay* in our position, to maintain our rank and dignity, to hold our office, our duty, or our calling, whatever it may be, but to bring *Christ* into all, to use them all for His glory. It is "as using the world and not abusing it." It is easy by one gigantic effort of the mind to give all up. It is hard to hold them, and yet use ALL for Christ. There is no cross in the other, there is the *daily* cross in this. The undetected hope of being *something* in the Church may suggest the one; nothing but the love of Christ can lead us to carry out the other. Let us see that the transformation be "according to the renewing of our minds," according to the Word, according to the Spirit of God, according to wisdom, judgment, and understanding. Let us see that it will *commend* the gospel of Christ to the conscience and not *disgust*. Let us see that it be *indeed* transformity to the world, transformity of the right kind, true, real, spiritual, heavenly.

And mark the effect: "that ye may *prove* what is that good and acceptable and perfect will of God." It is by thus being moulded by the Spirit of God that you will "prove" to your own satisfaction, to your joy and peace, and comfort and increase of faith, what it is that is good and acceptable and perfect, according to God's mind. You will thus know *what* the will of God is in everything, and it will be to you a good will, an acceptable and perfect will. You will have no doubt of it. You will prove it by the Spirit's testimony to your own heart. You will prove it and delight to do it; and it will be your joy and rejoicing.

Reader, do you know God's mercy to you as a lost sinner? Do you know it in having forgiven you all your sins?

Have you the Spirit's witness in your soul that He is *your* Saviour? Oh, what is Christ to you? Is He precious to you, or only a name without power?

Christian, beware of this present evil world, with its seductive influences on every side of you. Let it not mould you into its image. It surely will if you are not living very near to God. Beware of indecision. Be *wholehearted* for Christ. The bane of Christianity in this day is compromise, concession, expediency. These things are eating out its real life, and will leave it a *name* without any living power when the Lord comes. Beware! Watch, pray, live near to God! "Watch ye therefore, and pray always, that ye may be accounted worthy to escape all these things that shall come to pass, and to stand before the Son of man."

> Guide me, my Father! Thickly falls the night
>   Around my head.
> My heart is weary for the blessed light.
>   The path I tread
> May be the dark, drear vista of the tomb,
> For it is hidden in the gathering gloom.
>
> Guide me, my Father! other arms are weak
>   To lean upon;
> The strong and mighty Comforter I seek;
>   All else is gone!
> Oh for the everlasting arms to be,
> In my deep weakness, closely wrapped round me!
>
> Guide me, my Father, or my feet will stray
>   From Thee, my God,
> Will faltering leave the strait and thorn-strewed way
>   Which Jesus trod:
> I would be with Him where the holy meet;
> O Friend Omnipotent, guide Thou my feet!

> Guide me, my Father! Take my outstretched hand,
>   And lead me on,
> Until the mists and pitfalls of this land
>   Are ever gone;
> Until my spirit is at rest with Thee,
> From these dark griefs and dangers ever free.

FROM FAMILY PRAYERS.

AND since it is of Thy mercy, O gracious Father, that another day is added to our lives, we here dedicate both our souls and bodies to Thee and to Thy service, in a sober, righteous, and godly life: in which resolution do Thou, O merciful God, confirm and strengthen us; that as we grow in age, we may grow in grace, and in the knowledge of our Lord and Saviour, Jesus Christ.

FROM THE COMMUNION SERVICE.

AND here we offer and present unto Thee, O Lord, ourselves, our souls and bodies, to be a reasonable, holy, and living sacrifice unto Thee: humbly beseeching Thee, that we and all others who shall be partakers of this holy communion, may . . . be filled with Thy grace and heavenly benediction, and made one body with Him (Christ), that He may dwell in them, and they in Him.

The above extracts from the Form of Prayer to be used in Families and from the Communion Service of our Church, are so appropriate, and so fully embody and illustrate the doctrinal exposition of the preceding discourse, that we feel no apology is required for inserting them.—ED.

PAUL'S ADDRESS AT ANTIOCH.

Acts xiii, 16—41.

Then Paul stood up, and beckoning with *his* hand, said, Men of Israel, and ye that fear God, give audience. The God of this people of Israel chose our fathers, and exalted the people when they dwelt as strangers in the land of Egypt, and with an high arm brought he them out of it. And about the time of forty years suffered he their manners in the wilderness. And when he had destroyed seven nations in the land of Chanaan, he divided their land to them by lot. And after that he gave *unto them* judges about the space of four hundred and fifty years, until Samuel the prophet. And afterward they desired a king: and God gave unto them Saul the son of Cis, a man of the tribe of Benjamin, by the space of forty years. And when he had removed him, he raised up unto them David to be their king; to whom also he gave testimony, and said, I have found David the *son* of Jesse, a man after mine own heart, which shall fulfill all my will. Of this man's seed hath God, according to *his* promise, raised unto Israel a Saviour, Jesus: when John had first preached before his coming the baptism of repentance to all the people of Israel. And as John fulfilled his course, he said, Whom think ye that I am? I am not *he:* but, behold, there cometh one after me, whose shoes of *his* feet I am not worthy to loose. Men *and* brethren, children of the stock of Abraham, and whosoever among you feareth God, to you is the word of this salvation sent. For they that dwell at Jerusalem, and their rulers, because they knew him not, nor yet the voices of the prophets which are read every Sabbath Day, they have fulfilled *them* in condemning *him*. And though they found no cause of death *in him*, yet desired they Pilate that he should be slain. And when they had fulfilled all that was written of him, they took *him* down from the tree, and laid *him* in a sepulcher. But God raised him from the dead: and he was seen many days of them which came up with him from Galilee to Jerusalem, who are his witnesses unto the people. And we declare unto you glad tidings, how that the promise which was made unto the fathers, God hath fulfilled the same unto us their children, in that he hath raised up Jesus again; as it is also written in the second Psalm, Thou art my Son, this day have I begotten thee. And as concerning that he raised him up from the dead, *now* no more to return to corruption, he said on this wise, I will give you the sure mercies of David. Wherefore he saith also in another *Psalm*, Thou shalt not suffer thine Holy One to see corruption. For David, after he had served his own generation by the will of God, fell on sleep, and was laid unto his fathers, and saw corruption: but he, whom God raised again, saw no corruption.

Be it known unto you therefore, men *and* brethren, that through this man is preached unto you the forgiveness of sins: and by him all that believe are justified from all things, from which ye could not be justified by the law of Moses. Beware therefore, lest that come upon you which is spoken of in the prophets: Behold, ye despisers, and wonder, and perish: for I work a work in your days, a work which ye shall in no wise believe, though a man declare it unto you.

TRUE religion is large-hearted. The love of Christ has no bounds, no limits. It shone forth from the bosom of Jesus in all readiness to embrace the outskirts of fallen humanity. Wherever a soul could be found, there it would go; and the deeper fallen, the more deeply loved.

Every system of religion that does not go *out of itself* falls short of the true model. Every church, every denomination, yea, every soul that does not go out of itself, is unlike Christ. To wrap ourselves up in our own system to appropriate the promises and blessings of the Gospel exclusively to ourselves, without going out in largeness of heart to the utmost bounds of human kind in earnest desire to draw them into the same privilege, is one of the most palpable and widespread evidences of the fall of man, and one which still clings to God's people.

We see this principle in the opening words of this text. It contains a principle of universal application. "Men of Israel, *and ye that fear God.*" It is true, Israel is not forgotten, *must* not be. But while *our own* may come first, the stream must run on to the utmost bounds of the earth, wherever a God-fearing soul is to be found, and under whatever uniform.

"The God of this people of Israel *chose* our fathers, and *exalted* the people when they dwelt as *strangers in the land of Egypt.*" Three instructive points are brought before us in these words. God *chooses* His people. Those whom He chooses He "*exalts.*" And the people "chosen" and "exalted" are not chosen and exalted because of anything in themselves to recommend them, but simply because "they dwell as strangers in the land of Egypt."

We all, doubtless, know the application of this truth. It comes first in Paul's address, and should be *first* in every address. It is the foundation on which the superstructure is reared. Without this there is nothing. We were "strangers" to God. We were in "Egypt;" in bondage to a far worse taskmaster than Pharaoh, even "the prince of the power of the air." We were of those who "had no hope and were without God in this world." In this state God looked upon us. He "chose" us in Jesus. He "exalted" us in Jesus. Why? We cannot tell. His own wondrous love is the only answer. The depths of that love can never be sounded. Its heights can never be reached. Its breadth can never be grasped. It is unfathomable, unsearchable, unexplainable. "He loved me," and that is the only answer I can give to *any* question. But it *is* the answer, and the answer to *every* question. Those He "chose," He "exalted," and they were sinners, sinners of deepest dye, lost, ruined, undone. "Moreover, whom He did predestinate, them He also called: and whom

He called, them He also justified: and whom He justified, them He also glorified."

"And about the time of forty years suffered He their manners in the wilderness." The correct rendering of this verse is in the margin, and is very different from that which at first sight presents itself: "He bore or fed them, as a nurse beareth or feedeth her child." What a beautiful simile! The nurse bearing with the waywardness of the child; feeding them as *she* would feed the infant. What tenderness and compassion, what long-suffering and watchfulness, what care, consideration, and love! This was the history of Israel in the wilderness, and is the history of God's people now. What are *we*, and what is *He?* What have *we* been to *Him*, and what has *He* not been to *us?* Say, dear Christian reader. Can *you* not tell, even though every tongue on earth were silent? What has He been! "Wondrous grace, and love and compassion, every hour of the day!" What has He been! "Oh, angels cannot tell, thought cannot conceive, what He *has* been, nay, what He *is* to my soul!" See how the tender, watchful, loving nurse leads her child, removing every obstruction from its path, facing every danger first herself, and lovingly, yet wisely, giving to the child every choice portion that will make it happy. So God dealt with His people of old; so He deals with them now. Mark it here:—"And when He had *destroyed seven nations* in the land of Canaan, He *divided their land to them* by lot. And after that, *He gave unto them judges*, about the space of four hundred and fifty years, until Samuel the prophet."

"And afterward *they desired* a king: and God gave unto them Saul, the son of Cis, a man of the tribe of Benjamin, *by the space of forty years.* And when He had removed him, *He raised up unto them David* to be their king; to whom also He gave testimony, and said, I have found David, the son of Jesse, *a man after mine own heart, which shall fulfill all my will.* Of this man's seed hath God, *according to His promise*, raised unto Israel a Saviour, Jesus: when John had *first preached before His coming the baptism of repentance to all* the people of Israel."

Here we see the erring child crying out for its toy; Israel demanding a king. God answers their desire, though it was the rejection of *Him*. God chastises His people often by granting their foolish prayers, their sinful worldly desires. The answer proved a scourge to Israel, and for forty years delayed the blessing God had purposed to send them in raising up David. True, their sin could not *hinder* the blessing, but it could and did *delay* it. "According to promise" that blessing came, but not till after forty years' reaping the fruit of their sin. So it is now with God's people. God has in store for them every needful blessing. His blessings are "after His own heart." But they must look to Him for them. They must wait His time. This they will not do. They try to anticipate God. They run before Him. They plan, and carry out their plans. "They *desire*," and God answers their desires. Thus they defeat the very end they are aiming at. A blessing not "after His heart" is no blessing at all. A blessing that will not "fulfill *all* His will" must be eventually a curse. Thus we bring sorrow upon ourselves. Thus we *delay*, perhaps for "forty years," the blessing God had in store for us. Thus Israel made that wilderness, which was only a few days' journey, a wearisome march of forty years. Lord, what is man? Weak, wandering, foolish, sinful; always going *against* his very best interests;

always bringing trouble upon himself, and dishonor upon God.

And observe the Divine order here. Repentance *first* preached, and thus the way made ready for Jesus. So it is now; repentance first. But what is repentance? Sorrow for sin? No, no! This is the error of Rome, and of every anti-christian system. It is change of mind. Man must first change his thoughts about God, about himself, and about the way in which he is to be saved. Man's thought is, "I must do something to commend myself to God;" or "I must try and do better before I can expect to win His favor." He must change all these thoughts. God requires nothing from him. He gives him salvation freely, fully, now, and simply as a *sinner*. When man's thoughts are thus changed by the Holy Spirit, then *follows*—but not till then—sorrow for sin. Then Jesus comes and enters the heart thus prepared by the Spirit. He, like the Baptist of old, "goes before" the Lord, "to prepare His way." There is no real conversion to God without this. There never was; there never will be. Yet we are not to preach the Spirit. "*He* shall not speak of *Himself*." We are to preach Jesus. "He shall take of *mine*, and shall show it unto you." Jesus is to be our word, Jesus only. Come to Jesus. Come this very *moment*. Come *just as you are*. Wait for nothing, but come. Come! God bids you, Jesus welcomes you, the Spirit beseeches you. Why stand waiting? Your waiting implies that you are waiting *for something*. Thus you do not believe that *that* something has been done. You show by your hesitation and doubt that you do not yet believe that "your salvation is finished," that Jesus has *done* the work. You doubt Him, deny Him, set the seal of unbelief to the declarations of His word. You do it deliberately. The guilt of denying the Saviour's word and work is weighing upon you. You "make God a liar, because you believe not the *record* He has given of His Son."

"And as John fulfilled his course, he said, Whom think ye that I am? I am not He. But, behold, there cometh One after me, whose shoes of His feet I am not worthy to loose." Mark this, reader. John had a *course* to fulfill. So has every Christian minister, so has every Christian; so have you and I. We each stand in relation to God as he did. How did John fulfill that course? By bringing himself and those to whom he preached to the *test*. What was that test? It was how he stood in relation to *Christ*. "Whom think ye," he says, "that *I* am?" Have I been setting *myself* before you instead of *Christ?* Is Christ eclipsed, and is it *John* you see? No, "I am not He." Let me hide *myself.* Let Jesus be all. Direct your thoughts to *Him.* I am only a "voice," a "messenger." Ah, this was indeed *"fulfilling"* his course." The Christian or the Christian minister may be in his course, but is he *fully filling* it? Is he bringing himself and all his words and thoughts and ways to this test? Is he setting *himself* before men instead of Christ. Do those with whom he mingles think of him with such thoughts as should only be directed to Christ? How does he stand to others; how do others think of him? "What think ye of *Christ?*" Oh how many a Christian minister is robbing Christ of His glory, by taking to himself that honor and applause which belong only to Jesus! How is he secretly courting it by his preaching! How it gratifies him to be well spoken of! How he resents being eclipsed by another! And all this time, while ostensibly he is preaching *Jesus*, he is *really* preaching *himself*. And how many a congregation, too, is robbing Christ of His glory by putting it upon man! O Christian minister, test yourself; test yourself often, as John did. Say to yourself, say it in God's presence, with God's all-searching eye upon you, Who am I setting before my people? what do my people think of me? what place has *Christ* in it all? While ostensibly all is Jesus, am I not so shaping *myself*, my *sermons*, my *ministry*, as to catch the soft breath of human applause? Am *I* indeed only a "voice," heard but not seen! Oh self, self, self! How it predominates in many a Christian's heart! How we are living under its power, even under the humblest and holiest of all garbs, the name of Jesus! Christian, let your language, your conduct, your works and ways at all times say, "I am not He." Only thus will you *"fulfill* your course."

And mark the solemn reason for this. "Behold, there cometh One after me." Yes, Christian, whoever you are, Christ cometh after you. Then how are you preparing His way? What will He find in *your* course? Will He find *your*self or *Him*self? Oh solemnly, earnestly, I ask it, which? Which, Christian, which? He cometh after you. Surely He does. Will He find "wood, hay, stubble?" *or* will He find "gold, silver, precious stones?"

And in view of this solemn truth what should be your place? Just what John's was here. O God, grant that it may! "Whose shoes of His feet I am not worthy to loose." Yes, dear Christian reader, He is indeed "coming after you" in your "course." Oh under the solemn thought may you be found at His *"feet!"* Nay more, unworthy to be *there!* May the very *dust* Jesus treads upon be the *gold* of your life! May you be so hidden, *He* so precious, that none but He may ever be seen!

Mark, now, another truth! "For they that dwell at Jerusalem, and their rulers, *because they knew Him not,* nor yet *the voices of the prophets which are read every Sabbath-day,* they *have fulfilled them in condemning Him."* How man may hear the gospel every Sunday, and yet not know *Him!* How the truth may be read day by day, and yet the *voice* of the Spirit of God speaking in it may never be heard! And what does this *familiarity* with truth without the heart being brought under the power of it, lead to? To commit the greatest of all crimes, the murder of the Son of God. Familiarity with truth has the effect of *blinding* the heart, and of leading us into the commission of those very sins which it condemns. We may be hearing, day after day, the most awful denunciations on sin and sinners, and yet we ourselves be *unconsciously* the very sinners *described,* and doing the very sins *condemned.* It is in this way we have a fearful truth brought before us, namely, *that truth unreceived by the heart avenges itself by blinding the hearer, and allowing him to fall into sin.* This passage is an instance of it. Men who hear the truth know the truth, but those whose hearts are brought under the power of it little know what they are bringing upon themselves. Truth must *harden,* must *blind,* must make a man eventually insensible to sin, unless it be received into the heart by the power of the Spirit of God. We do not wonder, after years of listening to the truth, that men become insensible to the most earnest appeals, the most startling warnings. The heart and conscience have become hardened. "Ephraim is joined unto idols," and

God has uttered His solemn verdict from heaven, "let him alone." And what is the remedy for this state of things? The first word of this passage contains it, "because they knew *Him* not, nor the voices of the *prophets.*" It is to know *Christ*, as revealed in the word of God. Hearer of the truth, and yet unconverted, mark it well. You are "*dead,*" in the midst of all your religion. You are "without God," in the midst of all your knowledge. You are, you must be, till you know *Jesus*. To know *Him*, this is life, life everlasting. But only this.

"And though they found no cause of death in Him, yet *desired they* Pilate that He should be slain. And *when they had fulfilled all that was written* of Him, they took Him down from the tree, and laid Him in a sepulcher." Two truths are presented here. The first is, that enmity of heart was the cause of Christ's death. There was no cause of death, yet "they desired" it. "Out of the heart proceed murders." Here is the source of all evil. But let us not forget the second truth, that in all this work they were only fulfilling the Divine counsel. Faith looks behind the scene, and sees at every bend and turn in this diabolical act the work of God. This makes us calm when everything around us is going wrong. But if faith be not in exercise, if we are walking by sight, no wonder we are cast down and troubled. Nothing can live in the present scene but faith. Everything is out of course, and will be more so. But if each day we live within the veil; if we look at the "things unseen and eternal," we shall not be distracted. Lord, grant this to each one of Thy people, as the darkness thickens, and the midnight mists envelope us!

"But God raised Him from the dead, and *He was seen*

many days *of them which came up with Him from Galilee to Jerusalem, who are His witnesses unto the people.*" So must it be with each one of us. Would we see Jesus? We, too, must come up with Him from the sinful world to the heavenly Jerusalem. We must come up from the wilderness, "leaning on the Beloved." None see Him but those who come up with Him. They hold sweet fellowship with their risen Lord. They gaze into His heart of love. They hear His voice and see His countenance. To them He is "the chief of ten thousand, the altogether lovely." Their hearts give utterance again and again to the language of the loved one in the Canticles, "Let Him kiss me with the kisses of His mouth." They have left Galilee, and the heavenly Jerusalem is before them, and, precious thought! they are "coming up with *Him.*"

Not only so, but they are "His *witnesses* unto the people." Not the half-hearted Christian. Not the compromiser with the world. Not the one who knows little of Christianity beyond the name. No. These are no witnesses for God. These are disfigured and blotted "epistles," known indeed of men, but not known and read as God's living epistles. No, dear Christian reader, to be "*His* witnesses to the people," we must "come up *with Him*" from this wilderness. Our *back* must be on the world, our face toward the heavenly Jerusalem. Only thus shall we witness for God. Only thus shall we declare plainly that we "look for a city which hath foundations, whose builder and maker is God." This world has no foundations. It is the house built on the sand, and the storm is beginning to rise. But *that* city has "*foundations,*" yea, *many* foundations. It is stability itself, for it is the city of the living God, the "inheritance of the saints in light." O reader, is your eye on it? Is your *heart* in it? Are *you* "coming up with Jesus?" What witness are you giving for God, hour after hour, as you live here? Are you a *marked* man? Are you *wholly* on the Lord's side, or are you relaxing your *strictness*, and trying to meet the world half-way? A thousand times better err on the other side than on this. Christians are not *decidedly* on the Lord's side. Mark them, and beware of their example! If yours is not a *"peculiar"* path, a *marked* conduct, you are no "witness for Christ," though you *be* a Christian.

And now mark the great blessing flowing to us from the death and resurrection of the Lord Jesus. It is stated in one word. "I will give unto you the *sure* mercies of David." What streams of mercy now come down from that great source, and each one is endorsed with that precious covenant word, *"sure!"* "He hath made with me an everlasting covenant, ordered in all things, and *sure*." Every promise "sure." Every needful temporal blessing "sure." Everything in our daily lot provided for and "sure." "Not one good thing of all that the Lord our God has promised wanting;" and all "sure," because made sure by the death and resurrection of the Lord Jesus. The only "sure" thing on this side of heaven is that which is connected with Him.

But, unconverted reader, if grace is so full and free, there is a note of warning. "Beware therefore, lest that come upon you which is spoken in the prophets." In proportion to the fullness and freeness of the gospel, will be the guilt of rejecting it. Notwithstanding the "open door" of late years, and the great blessing that has attended the preaching of the Gospel, never has there been in the history of our world so much knowledge of God's word combined with so little of the power of godliness manifested in the life. Never has "the truth as it is in Jesus" been so trampled under foot as it is in these days. Let men call them "happy times" if they please, but they are "perilous times." And none of the judgments visited upon the nations of old can compare with the judgments with which this professing Christian nation will shortly be visited. They will be poured out without measure, and their record is in the Book of Revelation. May we take warning in time. Reader, and especially unconverted reader, "beware, lest *that* come upon you." You may smile incredulously at these warnings, but it is the smile of a man on the verge of a precipice. You are taking a step which can never be retraced. "Beware" then, and make sure of a refuge from the storm, by hiding in the clefts of the Rock of ages.

> O Jesus! the glory, the wonder and love
> Of angels and justified spirits above,
> And saints, who behold Thee not, yet dearly love,
>   Rejoicing in hope of Thy glory;
> Thou only, and wholly, art lovely and fair,
> Who robb'st not Jehovah, with Him to compare,
> Jehovah's own image glows in Thee; shines there
>   In visible bodily glory.
>   Worth divine dwells in Thee,
>   Excellent dignity,
>   Beauty and majesty,
>   Glory environs Thee;
> Power, honor, dominion, and life rest on Thee,
> O Thou chiefest among the ten thousands!
>
> Wherever we view Thee new glories arise;
> The man who's God's fellow, who rides on the skies,

Made flesh, dwelt among us; brought God to our eyes;
    In grace and truth showing His glory.
Thou spak'st to existence the heavens and their hosts,
The earth and its fullness, the seas and their coasts;
Time hangs on Thy word, and eternity boasts
    To crown and adorn Thee with glory.
      Worth, etc.

But how lovely dost Thou appear in our eyes,
When we view Thee incarnate in childhood's disguise,
Thy love's past all knowledge, while raptures surprise
    And ravish our hearts with Thy glory.
Thou in Thine own body, on th' accursed tree,
Did'st bear all our sins, while Thy God frowned on Thee,
Expiring in blood in our stead; and now we
    Exult in Thy merit and glory.
      Worth, etc.

Thy power all divine from the grave back again
Brought Thee, King of glory, Thou Lamb who wast slain!
First-born of the dead, crowned with honor supreme;
    Thy throne is established in glory.
There reign in Thy glory, O Thou great Adored!
Till Thy foes, crush'd under Thy feet, be no more;
Thy Throne shall triumph over all things restored,
    And eternity blaze with Thy glory.
      Worth divine dwells in Thee,
      Excellent dignity,
      Beauty and majesty,
      Glory environs Thee;
Power, honor, dominion, and life rest on Thee,
O Thou chiefest among the ten thousands!

THE PASSAGE OF THE JORDAN.

Joshua iii, 3, 4.

And they commanded the people, saying, When ye see the ark of the covenant of the LORD your God, and the priests the Levites bearing it, then ye shall remove from your place, and go after it: Yet there shall be a space between you and it, about two thousand cubits by measure: come not near unto it; that ye may know the way by which ye must go: for ye have not passed *this* way heretofore.

ONE of the most beautiful types of the Lord Jesus Christ in the Bible is the ark of the covenant. It is brought before our notice in the passage we have selected for consideration in connection with Joshua and the camp of Israel. The subject is beautifully instructive and eminently practical.

Joshua and the host of Israel have a great work before them, the passage of the Jordan, and the destruction of the guilty city of Jericho. Judgment was about to do its terrible work in the land. But mercy always precedes it. "He delighteth in mercy." "He willeth not the death of a sinner." Judgment came upon Jerusalem to the uttermost, but not till mercy had gone before, in a large and overflowing stream, in the person and work of the Son of God. Not till His tears had fallen upon her soil, and last of all His blood, was wrath poured out. It is so always with God. "I will sing of mercy and judgment," says the psalmist. But mercy is *first*. So was it with Jericho. Before Joshua and the host are allowed to take one step in the direction of judgment, grace is seen at work. Rahab in the doomed city hangs out the scarlet line, leans upon it as her only hope of safety, in dependence upon the promise made to her, and is safe in the hour of judgment. Thus we see mercy to the guilty; the safety of the trusting sinner, and, the source of it all, the scarlet line; all brought before us in the very midst of that scene over which the wrath of God was impending. How sweet to see that with our God this is always the *first* step, the background of the picture, bringing out in bold relief the righteousness of all His subsequent dealings.

The next thing we mark before one step is taken in the direction of judgment, is living faith in active exercise in the hearts of God's people. (See Josh. ii, 24.) These two features then are the Divine pencilings of the Spirit of God before He draws the darker lines of judgment; namely, grace before judgment, and faith before victory. These are, in one form or another, the background of every picture in the Bible where the darker colors of wrath are made to follow. Blessed be His name, who is "rich in mercy" and "the God of all grace," that it is so!

The next thing brought before us, in Divine and beautiful order, is the ark of the covenant. For if the streams of grace and faith run on before, where do they take their rise but in Him whom that ark represents, the Lord Jesus Christ? It is *He* that is to be the subject of all our praises; "for of Him and through Him and by Him are all things, who is over all, God blessed forever."

Mark, first, how Christ is exalted. "When ye see the ark of the covenant of the Lord your God, and the priests and the Levites bearing it, then ye shall remove from your place, and go after it." No matter *what* Israel might be doing, no matter how important, the moment the ark moved they were "to leave *their* place, and go after it." There was to be readiness of heart towards it. *It* was to have the first claim. The ark, the ark, *that* was to be the signal to the whole camp and to each member of it. The ark, *that* was to awaken in each heart a *response* and a *movement*. And the movement of that ark and its followers was only in one direction, towards the *promised land*. How clearly one eye was on that ark in after-days, and how ready to "remove from *his* place and go after it," was that man who exclaimed, "I am determined to know nothing among you save Jesus Christ and Him crucified:" "God forbid that I should glory, save in the cross of our Lord Jesus Christ, by whom the world is crucified unto me, and I unto the world."

Like the cloud of glory in the wilderness in earlier days, so was the ark now. Where *it* stood, the camp stood; when *it* moved, the camp went after it. So also Him whom they both represent: "And when He *putteth forth* His own sheep, He *goeth before them*, and the sheep *follow* Him, for they know His voice." So also with the redeemed in glory: "And when the *living creatures* went, the *wheels went by them:* and when the living creatures were lifted up from the earth, the wheels were lifted up. Whithersoever *the spirit* was to go, *they went*, thither was *their spirit* to go." "*When those stood, these stood;* when those went, these went, . . . for *the spirit of the living creatures* was in the wheels. And there was a *voice from the firmament that was over their heads,* when they stood, and had let down their wings." Mark it in later days: "For the Lamb which is in the midst of the throne shall feed them, and *shall lead them* to living fountains of waters, and God shall wipe away all tears from their eyes." "These are they which *follow the Lamb whithersoever He goeth.*"

"Ye shall remove from *your* place, and go after it." Reader, what is *your* place? I do not know. But this I say, if there be this day anything your heart is placing *before* Christ, anything you are placing *on a level* with Christ, God's word to you is, "Ye shall remove from *your* place, and go after *it.*" Is there anything *at this moment* which conscience tells you you are loving more than Him, any loved member of your family, any future prospect, any present plan, any way of your own which is of value to you? Is there *anything* that occupies more of your thoughts, and *consequently* more of your affections, than Christ does? Then I say, to *you* is this word sent, "Ye shall remove from your place, and go after it." Is there any place of amusement to which you are going, on which you cannot previously ask God's blessing, and which will not be the means of leading you nearer to Christ and to heaven? Is there any evening party at which you cannot speak for Christ? Is there any business transaction in which you are taking *secret advantage* over some *unsuspecting* tradesman? Is there any *secretly nourished* sin, any habitual cross temper or sour disposition, anything in *you* before *others* that is contrary to the mind of the holy Jesus? Then I say, to *you* is the word from God this day, "Ye shall *remove* from *your* place, and *go after it.*"

Oh solemn, searching word for all! For Rationalism,

with its sophistry, setting up the human understanding in the place of Christ. For Ritualism, by fascinating ceremonial, hiding Christ. For Evangelicalism, with its scriptural *form*, but lack of *spiritual life* and *power*, equally hiding Christ. For *individual* Christianity, ever treading the *dead level*, the *beaten path* of Christians around, without the *distinctive* mark of the life and love and power of the Spirit of God raising them above it so as to distinguish them as Christ was distinguished. To each one comes the word of God now as to Israel of old, "Ye shall remove from your place, and go after it."

"Yet there shall be a space between you and it, about two thousand cubits by measure: come not near unto it, that ye may know the way by which ye must go: for ye have not passed this way heretofore." The reason of the space between the ark and the camp was that every eye might see it. If it had not been far *in advance*, it could not have been seen by those in the background. Therefore the necessity for a space between of two thousand cubits. This was the great design of God, that *each one* of the mighty moving throng should see it *for himself*. One object alone engaged the thoughts and occupied the attention as they moved onward, the ark. Not the Levites who bore it, or the equipage, however beautiful, but the ark itself. Surely this has a lesson for us! Christ must be very conspicuous. The eye of every one of God's chosen should be on Him and Him only. He should be so clearly presented to every soul that the weakest, the feeblest, the blindest in the ranks, though they may be able to see nothing else, may see Him.

And why? "That ye may know the way by which ye must go." If Israel had not seen that ark, if the eye had rested on anything else, they must have lost their way. "There is none other name given among men whereby we must be saved but the name of Jesus." It might have seemed narrow or exclusive to make the question of inheriting or losing the land dependent upon looking to the ark, but so it was. It was God's appointment, and whoever looked not to it forfeited the inheritance. Just so is it now. Men are making many ways to heaven. Latitudinarianism is for setting aside the cross of Christ as narrow and exclusive. Men are beginning to think that, do what they may, or live as they please, it will somehow be all right at last. Ah! if the ark be not before them, and the eye of faith resting upon it, the end will be that the waters of judgment will overwhelm them. Only one way; that is, Jesus.

And mark the warning. "Come not *near* unto it." Any one coming near to that ark hid it *by his own person* from the view of others. Thus it is that *self* in any form obscures the glory of the Lord Jesus. How often instead of Christ man is seen! How often the shadow of *something* is between the eye of faith and Christ the true ark! How stealthily the flesh gains ground and comes near to the ark, so that our true joy and peace and glory are hidden! Oh retire from view! Fall back into the ranks and let nothing be seen but the ark. Let self in every form, good and bad, go out of sight. Make the way between your soul and Jesus very clear. Let nothing, however valued, come between. Let the eye rest undividedly on Jesus. Then will you see the way before you. You will walk in the right path. You will go through the dark waves of sorrow and trial without fear. You will conquer the foe, however "great and strong." Faith will triumph, and you will raise your trophy of victory as a memorial of the loving-kindness of the Lord from the very waves that threatened to overwhelm you.

"For ye have not passed this way heretofore." Dear Christian reader, whatever may have been your experience of the past, the way *before* you is untried. You know not what it may be. Oh trust it not! It is still the wilderness. It is still a deceitful heart you carry. It is still the deep darkness and the dreary mist of the last watch of the night. Look now more than ever to Jesus, Jesus only. "Ye have not passed this way heretofore." Be sure that the eye of faith is steadily fixed on the ark. Be sure that Christ is the undivided object of your affections, in all things, great and small. "Ye have not passed this way heretofore." Then beware of anything coming between your soul and Jesus. Look not to *man*, not even to *good* men. Cease from man altogether. Have no confidence in the flesh. All fail when put to the test. Only Christ is "faithful and true." The soul that trusts in aught else than Jesus is trusting a bruised reed, and will soon feel the piercings of disappointment and sorrow. Oh look only to Jesus! You have proved Him, and tried Him, and found Him faithful. Is *He* not worthy of *all* your trust?

Mark one truth more brought before us in connection with the passage of the Jordan. "And it came to pass, when all the people were clean passed over Jordan, that the Lord spake unto Joshua, saying, Take you twelve men out of the people, out of every tribe a man, and command ye them, saying, Take you hence out of the midst of Jordan, out of the place *where the priests' feet stood firm*, twelve stones, and ye shall carry them over with you, and leave them in the lodging place where ye shall lodge this night." What were these stones for? One for every tribe! representing the whole congregation of Israel. They were to be taken out of the midst of the waters of death; they were to be reared up on the other side, as trophies of *victory*. They told their tale, how that Israel had come up out of the place of death and judgment. They were standing memorials of victory over death. This, too, in the country which as yet was in the enemy's hands. The rams' horns had not yet been blown. The walls of Jericho still stood formidably before them. The inheritance was not yet in possession. Still they had the witness of resurrection-life among them, the victory over death.

So is it now with the Church of God. We are still in the enemy's land. Its walls and bulwarks are still before us. "The kingdoms of this world" have not yet become "the kingdoms of our Lord Jesus Christ." The inheritance is yet in reserve. But, blessed be God, the Ark has been down in the waters of death. He has brought us up "with Him," into resurrection-life. We have gotten the victory. We have this victory, this resurrection-life, even in the very land of the enemy. Soon the inheritance will be in possession. Soon the shout will be heard that shall shake the walls of "this present world" to the ground. The guilty Jericho was never to rise again. This world of sin and guilt, of sorrow and trial, of bondage and misery, shall pass away forever. Soon shall be seen "the King in His beauty." "His servants shall serve Him;" and "sorrow and sighing shall flee away."

"Come, Lord Jesus, come quickly!" Christian, be ready. The time is at hand, the hour draws near.

Another week may not pass before you see the Lord. Keep your garments. Live near to Jesus. Especially live much *alone* with God. It is the only safe place here. There is no time now for anything else save to win souls to Christ and to live near to God. O reader, may it be thy work and thy place, "till the shadows flee away!" "Behold, I come as a thief. Blessed is he that watcheth, and keepeth his garments, lest he walk naked, and they see his shame."

>Nothing between, Lord, nothing between;
> Let me Thy glory see;
> Draw my soul close to Thee,
> Then speak in love to me:
>   Nothing between.

>Nothing between, Lord, nothing between;
> Let not earth's din and noise
> Stifle Thy still small voice;
> In it let me rejoice:
>   Nothing between.

>Nothing between, Lord, nothing between;
> Nothing of earthly care,
> Nothing of tear or prayer,
> No robe that self may wear:
>   Nothing between.

>Nothing between, Lord, nothing between;
> Unbelief disappear,
> Vanish each doubt and fear,
> Fading when Thou art near:
>   Nothing between.

>Nothing between, Lord, nothing between;
> Shine with unclouded ray,
> Chasing each mist away,
> O'er my whole heart bear sway:
>   Nothing between.

Nothing between, Lord, nothing between;
    Thus may I walk with Thee,
    Thee only may I see,
    Thine only let me be:
            Nothing between.

Nothing between, Lord, nothing between;
    Till Thine eternal light,
    Rising on earth's dark night,
    Bursts on my open sight:
            Nothing between.

Nothing between, Lord, nothing between;
    Till, the last conflict o'er,
    I stand on Canaan's shore,
    With Thee forevermore:
            Nothing between.

THE SYRIAN LEPER.

2 KINGS v, 1–19.

Now Naaman, captain of the host of the king of Syria, was a great man with his master, and honorable, because by him the Lord had given deliverance unto Syria: he was also a mighty man in valor; *but he was* a leper. And the Syrians had gone out by companies, and had brought away captive out of the land of Israel a little maid; and she waited on Naaman's wife. And she said unto her mistress, Would God my lord *were* with the prophet that *is* in Samaria! for he would recover him of his leprosy. And *one* went in, and told his lord, saying, Thus and thus said the maid that *is* of the land of Israel. And the king of Syria said, Go to, go, and I will send a letter to the king of Israel. And he departed, and took with him ten talents of silver, and six thousand *pieces* of gold, and ten changes of raiment. And he brought the letter to the king of Israel, saying, Now, when this letter is come unto thee, behold, I have *therewith* sent Naaman my servant to thee, that thou mayest recover him of his leprosy. And it came to pass, when the king of Israel had read the letter, that he rent his clothes, and said, *Am* I God, to kill and to make alive, that this man doth send unto me to recover a man of his leprosy? Wherefore consider, I pray you, and see how he seeketh a quarrel against me.

And it was *so*, when Elisha the man of God had heard that the king of Israel had rent his clothes, that he sent to the king, saying, Wherefore hast thou rent thy clothes? let him come now to me, and he shall know that there is a prophet in Israel. So Naaman came with his horses and with his chariot, and stood at the door of the house of Elisha. And Elisha sent a messenger unto him, saying, Go and wash in the Jordan seven times, and thy flesh shall come again to thee, and thou shalt be clean. But Naaman was wroth, and went away, and said, Behold, I thought, He will surely come out to me, and stand, and call on the name of the Lord his God, and strike his hand over the place, and recover the leper. *Are* not Abana and Pharpar, rivers of Damascus, better than all the waters of Israel? may I not wash in them, and be clean? So he turned, and went away in a rage. And his servants came near, and spake unto him, and said, My father, *if* the prophet had bid thee *do some* great thing, wouldest thou not have done *it?* how much rather, then, when he saith to thee, Wash, and be clean? Then he went down, and dipped himself seven times in Jordan, according to the saying of the man of God: and his flesh came again like unto the flesh of a little child, and he was clean.

And he returned to the man of God, he and all his company, and came and stood before him: and he said, Behold, now I know that *there is* no God in all the earth, but in Israel; now therefore, I pray thee, take a blessing of thy servant. But he said, *As* the Lord liveth, before whom I now stand, I will receive none. And he urged him to take *it;* but he refused. And Naaman said, Shall there not then, I pray thee, be given to thy servant two mules' burden of earth? for thy servant will henceforth offer neither burnt-offering nor sacrifice unto other gods, but unto the Lord. In this thing the Lord pardon thy servant, *that* when my master goeth into the house of Rimmon to worship there, and he leaneth on my hand, and I bow myself in the house of Rimmon: when I bow down myself in the house of Rimmon, the Lord pardon thy servant in this thing. And he said unto him, Go in peace. So he departed from him a little way.

THE history of Naaman is one of the most remarkable in God's Word. It brings before our notice two striking features of human character frequently found united, human greatness and human misery. Along with these it develops that which is the secret cause of all our misery, pride.

Let us look at it; and, with the light of God's Holy Spirit, learn solemn and holy lessons.

If you go down deep enough into any heart, you will discover some secret sorrow, and at the root of that sorrow you will often find some secret sin. "Now Naaman, captain of the host of the king of Syria, was a great man with his master, and honorable, because by him the Lord had given deliverance unto Syria: he was also a mighty man in valor, *but he was a leper.*" Such was Naaman, a great man, mighty in valor, honorable, a deliverer of others from bondage, one who had won golden laurels, "*but he was a leper.*"

How affecting are the words, "but he was a leper!" Ah, in every record of human greatness, in every cup of honor, in every sunny picture of human life, there comes, *at the end* a " but," something to shade or sadden; some thorn in the path piercing our feet and making our secret hearts bleed, while the garlands of human applause glitter on the brow! They are down in the heart of almost every man, mocking the smile that would force its way to the countenance. Many of the smiles of human life are but the glittering actors on a stage, beneath which lies a smouldering volcano.

So it was with Naaman. Wherever he went he carried with him a wasting disease, exposing him to the rude gaze of the passer by. In the grandeur which accompanied him, there was a pressing sorrow weighing down the heart beneath its load.

What a picture of multitudes! Gay, brilliant, happy, honorable before the world, the envy or the pride of thousands, and yet in themslves restless, unsatisfied, weary. There is a secret worm gnawing at the heart, and making man ill at ease while surrounded with all the grandeur and luxury of life. The moral leprosy of man, the hidden cause of all his sorrow and misery, is *sin*.

Now let us notice how God dealt with this man to remove his leprosy and make him happy, and see in it an exact picture of the way in which He acts in removing man's sin and giving him peace.

The first means brought before us is " the little maid." "And she said unto her mistress, Would God my lord were with the prophet that is in Samaria! for he would recover him of his leprosy." Mark how she speaks. She *knows of the great healer in Israel.* She *longs* for the leper to be healed. She knows that he will be healed, if he will only go. She speaks the language of *confidence.* Who is it speaks thus? A little waiting-maid. Oh how God brings our great thoughts down! How He "chooses the base things of this world, yea, and things that are not, to bring to nought things that are." "I thank Thee, O Father, Lord of heaven and earth, that Thou hast hid these things from the wise and prudent, and hast revealed them to *babes.*" Yes, a little waiting-maid beholds the leprous sinner, longs for his salvation, knows Christ's willingness to heal, and of the perfect cure for sin!

Mark, again, through what little things God accomplishes His wondrous works. The whole of this cure He builds on the word of a little maid! "Give me to drink;" what a little word, and yet see what God built on it, the conversion of one guilty soul, and through her the drawing of multitudes to hear the words of life from the Saviour's own lips! Lot's wife is turned into a pillar of salt by a *look;* the world created by a *word;* man ruined by an *apple;* a great nation humbled to the dust by a *worm,* an *east wind,* a *gourd,* a *fish;* a guilty land destroyed by an *insect;* a leper healed by a *touch;* a wandering disciple restored to the fold by *the crowing of a cock;* a loving heart, rent with sorrow, by *the sounding of her own name* restored to fullness of joy! How wonderful! and yet how different from us. To accomplish great ends, we use great means. God does exactly the reverse. And why? Because *our* ends are accomplished by the means we use. God's are not. And that is God's object in this? That we should mark not the *visible end,* but the *invisible will;* not the *process*, but the *Hand* that is working; not the things *seen and temporal*, but the *mighty Worker unseen and eternal.* As creatures of *sense* we are arrested by the *visible ends.* God would have us see, not *them*, but *Him;* and therefore He works by the weakest means, in order that, by *observing the great disproportion between the means and the end,* we may recognize His hand.

But let us mark another striking feature in this narrative. Observe what implicit confidence both the *king* and *Naaman* place in the little maid's word. It must surely have been Divinely overruled that just at this critical moment both the one and the other should have listened to, and acted upon, the words of a mere child! But when God is about to do His work, He so orders outward circumstances that they shall bring about His ends. He not only changes external circumstances so as to meet our spiritual state, but He changes our spiritual state that it shall meet those circumstances. *Adaptation* is God's great law, both in nature and providence. And He so adapts *external* circumstances to our spiritual state, and our spiritual state to external circumstances, that His great end is accomplished.

We mark this further in the case of Naaman. If this message had come *shortly after* he had become a leper, he might probably have neglected it; but long years of internal misery and the heavy pressure of disease had brought him down, and made him willing to listen to any proposal of cure. How often we have heard the message, "Come to Christ;" but we did not go. God has made our burdens press more heavily, has so emptied us from one vessel to another, that we are broken. Then, how willing to listen! Then, with the humbled spirit of a child, we come and bow at the Saviour's feet. But oh, what a process God has had to employ to bring us to this! What long years of discipline! What waves of sorrow rolling over our heads? what withering of earthly gourds! what breaking of human cisterns! what tear-dimmed eyes and bleeding hearts! And what has all this been for? To bring us to listen, like a child, to the message from heaven, and to take, as poor bankrupt sinners, the gift of eternal life.

Let us notice now, in the case of Naaman, how the pride of the natural heart works, and learn from it what is the sinner's greatest hindrance in obtaining salvation. Mark how simple had been the message. "Go to the prophet." And Naaman prepares to obey. But observe how the simplicity of the message is encumbered. Naaman goes first to the king of Syria, and the king of Syria writes a letter to the king of Israel. Then he takes horses, chariots, silver, gold, changes of raiment, and thus he sets out.

And is not this the exact picture of the human heart? "Come to Christ," is the simple message to the sinner. "Just as you are and without one plea." The message is clear, the invitation to all. But see how he sets about it! See what a hill he makes for himself to get up! See what a long, tedious way he makes for himself! See what he prepares to take with him! See how he resolves to be better, how he intends to pray, how he determines to break off some of his sins, what alms he purposes giving, what a good life he makes up his mind to lead, with what earnestness he sets about taking with him a number of things like these, in order to get into the favor of God! Just like Naaman. The simple and straight road to Christ is not to his mind, and he sets off in his own.

And why was this? Naaman wanted to be healed, but he wanted to be healed in his own way. He wanted to be cleansed, but in a way suited to his own dignity. He could not come to the door of the prophet without any letter of recommendation from the king, without his chariot and horses, without his silver and gold and raiment. Oh no! That would be beneath his dignity. That would be to come like a beggar! And *that* the pride of the natural heart could not brook.

Oh how like man at all times! To come to Christ, renouncing everything; to come poor, blind, leprous, and as beggars to the gate of heaven; the sinner's pride cannot brook this. He goes to SELF first, before he goes to Christ, and so self always leads him wrong, No; go just as you are, straight to Jesus. Go with nothing; go as a beggar; go feeling that you deserve only one thing at God's hands, and that is condemnation. Those who go emptiest, come away the fullest. Those who go with a burden of sin, come away with joy and gladness. Take nothing to recommend you. You *want* riches, take none with you. You *want* a righteous robe, take none of your own patched-up garments with you. Come as you are. The greater the sinner, the greater your need of the Saviour. Your sin is your claim to His mercy. Your wretchedness is your most powerful plea. Your guilt and ruin are your strongest recommendation. These are pleas almighty, and ever prevail. These find a way to the Saviour's ear and a Saviour's heart when nothing else can. These are your passport to His throne at all times. These, and only these, draw from the lips of mercy to the ear of misery the joyous word, the sweetest sound on this side of heaven in a sinner's ear, " I will; be thou clean."

So Naaman, with his princely equipage and costly presents, starts off with the letter to the king of Israel. There he meets with no success. The king is in a rage with the message and the messenger. Oh how would all this humiliation have been spared to Naaman had he gone straight to Elisha!

> "Weary, working, burdened one,
>   Why toil you so?
> 'It is finished,' all was done,
>   Long, long ago.
>
> Till to Jesus' work you cling,
>   By a simple faith,
> Doing is a deadly thing,
>   Doing ends in death.
>
> Cast thy deadly doing down,
>   Down at Jesus' feet;
> Stand in Him—in Him alone,
>   Gloriously complete."

Still this "weary, working, burdened one" must go simply to Christ. God will not abate one iota of His message to meet the sinner's case. Again the word comes to Naaman, "Let him come now to me, and he shall know that there is a prophet in Israel." Yes, God's cry to the "toiling one" is, Come to Christ. It is a simple, royal road for poor wandering sinners.

Again Naaman starts off, and stands with his train and his presents at the prophet's door. Why did he not do this at *first*, and "without money and without price"? He had made a short and simple journey a long and tedious and humiliating one. And what does he expect God's messenger to do? "Surely he will come out to me." Surely with such a train, and such presents, he will honor me! Surely now there is that about me which must command the healing I seek!

No; the "great man" and "honorable" is left standing outside at the door! The prophet remains in his chamber, and simply *sends* out a message *by his servant.* He does not even condescend to look upon the "great man," or notice his presents. He treats with inhospitality, the man whom he had invited to "come to him," and sends him from his door with a short, abrupt message! Oh how humiliating to the "great man's" pride! How God casts all the "money and price" of the natural heart to the ground!

And does this conduct on the part of Elisha startle us? Does this treatment show that God does not love the poor leprous sinner? No, His heart yearns over him with inconceivable, unutterable love. But God will not stoop to *your* way of being saved. You must adopt *His.* The voice is, "Wash, and be clean." But if you choose to take your own way of being saved instead of His; if you prefer to "work and toil" to make yourself worthy, instead of coming and taking His salvation as a free gift; if you persist in taking a course He has not set before you, to listening to His voice and obeying it, He will not stoop to you. He will humble you. He will empty you of your fine thoughts and ways. He will rebuke you, and lay you very low in the dust. He will treat you as Elisha did Naaman at the door of his house, as a *beggar.* He will not *look* at you, or your fine load of self-righteousness you bring with you. The healing is ready, the health is ready, the pardon is ready, the joy is ready, the peace is ready, the crown and glory are ready, all full, and free, and yours, just as you are. But if you choose to reject, if you turn away because of the terms, if you cannot come down *to His feet,* if you cannot stoop to be humbled, then you go on, and you die in your sins.

Mark the confirmation of this in the case of Naaman. "And Elisha sent a messenger unto him, saying, Go wash in Jordan seven times, and thy flesh shall come again to thee, and thou shalt be clean. But Naaman was wroth, and went away, and said, "Behold, I thought, He will surely come out to me, and stand, and call on the name of the Lord, his God, and strike his hand over the place, and recover the leper. Are not Abana and Pharpar, rivers in Damascus, better than all the waters of Israel? May I not wash in them, and be clean? So he turned and went away in a rage."

We observe Naaman's sin: he thought he ought to have been treated in a way more worthy of his dignity. He despised the means to which he was directed. He thought much more highly of other means. He was wounded that his own thoughts and ways of being healed had been so completely set aside.

So is it with the sinner. He does not like to be treated as if he was so very bad. He would rather be treated as if he were *somebody* before God. He has a higher estimate of *his own means* of being saved than he has of *God's*. So the pride of his heart rebels, and he turns away.

Well, God will not relax. You *must* come to God's way. God will never descend to yours.

So the servants draw near and expostulate with him. He who had arranged all outward events to meet the spiritual state of the leper; He who so ordered it that the king of Syria and Naaman should listen to the words of a "little maid," had so arranged that at this critical moment, on which the whole matter seemed to hinge, Naaman should be met by his *servants*, the *humble* ones again being used by God to carry out God's purposes of grace.

Yes, God makes outward events change to suit our spiritual state, and our spiritual state to change, so as to meet outward events. Thus, He carries out at all times His great designs of sovereign grace.

So, by God's gracious *interference*, nothing else, the leper was led to *God's* way from *his own*. He went and washed, according to the saying of the man of God, and "his flesh came again, like unto the flesh of a little child, and he was clean." "The flesh of a little child;" this was the "new nature." "Except a man be *born again*, he cannot see the kingdom of God." Now, all the effects of that new nature begin to show themselves. Now he knows that only the God of Israel is the God. Now he knows that there is none like Him. Now He would offer a blessing, not to *procure* salvation, but as an offering of gratitude and love. But no; Elisha will not take this. Why? To let Naaman see that nothing of Naaman's has had any hand in the work of healing. It has all been grace. It has all come to the poor leper without money and without price. Had Elisha taken the reward, the weak conscience of Naaman might have said, "Well, I have given him something for it." The Spirit of God is very jealous of Christ's glory. He will let Naaman know that all is grace, and that the flesh has no place in His sight. So God is glorified, and the leper is filled with humble, grateful praises. As a poor sinner, he has nothing to say now, but "worthy the Lamb."

Now mark another effect of the new nature. It is tenderness of conscience. See it in Naaman. "In this thing the Lord pardon thy servant, that when my master goeth into the house of Rimmon to worship there, and he leaneth on my hand, and I bow myself in the house of Rimmon:

when *I bow myself in the house of Rimmon, the Lord pardon thy servant in this thing.*"

Tenderness of conscience is ever the fruit of the new nature. We tremble because the Spirit of God is in us. At every step we challenge ourselves; and at every step, too, the tender conscience cries out, "Lord, pardon Thy servant." Yes, these are the "fruits of the Spirit." Conscience is tender; for God is before the soul in all His glory.

But mark Elisha's reply. He says not, "Go." He says not, "Do *not* go." He leaves the conscience of the renewed one alone with God. He leaves it to act before God, under the power of that Spirit that had awakened it; well knowing that "He who had begun a good work would perfect it." He speaks the word of his Master, "Go in peace." He leaves the awakened conscience of the washed soul to act under its own responsibility to God, and whispers over it the word of heaven, "Peace."

Unconverted reader, "wash, and be clean." God's voice to you is not "work," not "do," but "wash," "wash," "*wash*, and be clean." It is not "*keep on* washing till you become *cleaner.*" No. It is "*wash*, and be clean." It is a washing that once and forever fits the soul for God's presence. Sinner, cast every thought and every way of thine own to the winds. Take God's and leave thine own forever. "Wash, and be clean." Remember the solemn words of the Lord Jesus to *thy* soul, "If I wash thee not, thou hast *no part with me.*"

> Not what I am, O Lord, but what Thou art!
> That, that alone can be my soul's true rest;
> Thy love, not mine, bids fear and doubt depart,
> And stills the tempest of my tossing breast.

THE SYRIAN LEPER.

Thy name is Love! I hear it from yon cross;
   Thy name is Love! I read it on yon tomb;
And meaner love is perishable dross,
   But this shall light me through time's thickest gloom.

It blesses now, and shall forever bless,
   It saves me now, and shall forever save;
It holds me up in days of helplessness,
   It bears me safely o'er each swelling wave.

'Tis what I know of Thee, my Lord and God,
   That fills my soul with peace, my lips with song;
Thou art my health, my joy, my staff, my rod,
   Leaning on Thee in weakness, I am strong.

I am all want and hunger: this faint heart
   Pines for a fullness which it finds not here;
Dear ones are leaving, and, as they depart,
   Make room within for something yet more dear.

More of Thyself, oh, show me hour by hour,
   More of Thy glory, O my God and Lord;
More of Thyself in all Thy grace and power,
   More of Thy love and truth, Incarnate Word!

THE ASCENDED SAVIOUR AND HIS GIFTS TO THE CHURCH.

Ephesians iv, 1—16.

I therefore, the prisoner of the Lord,) beseech you, that ye walk worthy of the vocation wherewith ye are called, with all lowliness and meekness, with long-suffering, forbearing one another in love; endeavoring to keep the unity of the Spirit in the bond of peace. *There is* one body, and one Spirit, even as ye are called in one hope of your calling; one Lord, one faith, one baptism, one God and Father of all, who *is* above all, and through all, and in you all. But unto every one of us is given grace according to the measure of the gift of Christ. Wherefore he saith, When he ascended up on high, he led captivity captive, and gave gifts unto men. (Now that he ascended, what is it but that he also descended first into the lower parts of the earth? He that descended is the same also that ascended up far above all heavens, that he might fill all things.) And he gave some, apostles; and some, prophets; and some, evangelists; and some, pastors and teachers; for the perfecting of the saints, for the work of the ministry, for the edifying of the body of Christ; till we all come in the unity of the faith, and of the knowledge of the Son of God, unto a perfect man, unto the measure of the stature of the fullness of Christ; that we *henceforth* be no more children, tossed to and fro, and carried about with every wind of doctrine, by the sleight of men, *and* cunning craftiness, whereby they lie in wait to deceive; but, speaking the truth in love, may grow up into him in all things, which is the head, *even* Christ; from whom the whole body fitly joined together and compacted by that which every joint supplieth, according to the effectual working in the measure of every part, maketh increase of the body, unto the edifying of itself in love.

WHAT a comprehensive and instructive portion of God's word is that now before us! It is one of the addresses delivered by Paul when in prison; and it would seem as if the apostle spoke from his dungeon chains with a power and an earnestness which only "fellowship with Christ's sufferings" can impart to the heart and pen. Let us listen to his words, and strive to catch the echo of his voice, as the Spirit of God speaks through it in solemn, earnest, searching tones.

We mark again the word "therefore," showing us a connection with some previous utterance. This connection is not with the *third* chapter, but with the closing verses of the *second* chapter. The third chapter is (excepting the first verse) in a parenthesis. At the end of the first verse the apostle enters on explanatory matters, and in the first verse of our present chapter begins where he had broken off. There are many instances in St. Paul's letters of this parenthetic style, and the reader would do well to notice them, lest they prevent his seeing clearly the apostle's line of thought.

"I therefore, the prisoner of the Lord, beseech you that ye walk worthy of the vocation wherewith ye are called." And why? Mark the connection of the word "therefore" with the closing verses of the second chapter, and we shall then see the reason. "In whom ye also are builded together *for an habitation of God through the Spirit:*" therefore "walk *worthy* of the vocation."

But how? "With *all lowliness* and meekness, with long-suffering, forbearing one another in love." It is as if the apostle would say, "You are God's *habitation.* He dwells in you. Therefore be very lowly, meek, long-suffering, forbearing." This is the way to "walk worthy." Mark a corresponding passage, Philippians ii, 12, 13, and assigning for humble walking the same motive, an indwelling and inworking God. Therefore the need of watchfulness and prayer lest the flesh should work, and not God; lest we should run before Him, and so take the matter out of God's hands into our own. Oh, what need of constant, wakeful, watchful, prayerful waiting upon God, for with the flesh cleaving to every thought and word and deed, every motive and plan and duty, we are never out of the place of danger! May our prayer, dear reader, always be "Hold Thou me up, and I shall be safe:" "Search me, O God, and know my heart: try me, and know my thoughts; and see if there be any wicked way in me, and lead me in the way everlasting."

The next subject the apostle brings before us is the unity of the Church. The Church is one. The Father, the Son, the Holy Ghost, and the Church are all *one*. The Church proceeds out of the Triune Godhead, "which were born, not of blood, nor of the will of the flesh, nor of the will of man, but of God." Just as of old the cherubim and the mercy-seat were made out of *one* and *the same* piece of beaten work, so the Church is the body of the Godhead. We have the same truth brought before us in the living creatures of the Prophet Ezekiel. "Also *out of the midst of the fire* came the likeness of four living creatures. And this was their appearance; they had the likeness of *a man*" (Ezek. i, 5). We see the living Church coming out of the *fire*, the symbol of the Triune God. Not only so, but we see whose image this God-born Church bears; "they had the likeness of *a man*," even the man Christ Jesus. The "living creatures" are here a picture of the Church *in glory*, made like unto Christ. So the Apostle John also shows us, "we shall be *like Him*, for we shall see Him as He is." Connected with this *first* "likeness of a *man*" is the likeness of the "lion," the "ox," the "eagle:" but the "man" is *first*. It shows us that the animal creation will be blessed and exalted by connection with this man Christ Jesus. It was cursed because of the first man's sin: it shall be blessed because of the second man's redemption. "For we know that the whole creation groaneth and travaileth in pain together until now;" "the creature itself also shall be delivered from the bondage of corruption into the glorious liberty of the children of God."

Still, though the Church and the Triune God are *one*, we are besought to "*keep* the unity." This is the prayer of our blessed Lord for all His people (John xvii). We *are* one. We are to aim to *keep* one. And yet all in "the Spirit."

And we notice how all is traced up to God the Father. There is "union," "peace," the "body," the "Spirit," the "hope," "faith," "baptism," the "Lord:" all are made to culminate in "God the Father," who is "*above* all" as to His Godhead, "through all" as to His operations, "in you all" as to His indwelling.

From this ascended God-man, Christ Jesus, every blessing comes down. There is "grace given to *every one* of us." The weakest and feeblest, the most peculiar, the most infirm and helpless, the one least thought of by the Church or the world; not *one* lacks the blessing from on high.

We have a beautiful commentary on these words in the Old Testament. "Behold, how good and how pleasant it is for brethren to dwell together in *unity!* It is like the *precious ointment* upon *the head*, that ran down upon the beard, even Aaron's beard: that went down to the *skirts* of his garments" (Psalm cxxxiii). We notice the precious ointment, the emblem of the Holy Spirit, on the head of Aaron, going down to the very *skirts* of the garment. So does the Holy Spirit come down from our ascended High Priest, Christ Jesus, to the least and to the lowliest of the body. With such a Spirit poured out from on high on each of the Lord's little ones, there must be unity, even "the unity of the Spirit." Such union must indeed be "good and pleasant." There is in it the *fragrance* and *perfume* of the "precious ointment." It is in each member "a sweet savor of Christ," binding heart to heart in indissoluble bonds, and leaving an impression for God. Oh that it were more manifest in our Churches and in our families, and were poured out in large measure on our own souls individually! The character of the last days, in one of its saddest forms, will be, "without natural affection;" and again, "these be they who *separate* themselves, *sensual*, having not the Spirit." O reader, let nothing induce you to be on discordant or unhappy terms with any member of your family or with any one of God's people around you! Ask for a larger measure of God's Spirit on your soul, that you may *stoop*, that you may sacrifice your own claims, *even though right*, and be able to banish the distant look, or reserve, or frown on the brow of one *near* to you? Let the Spirit of God make you *united*, and bind your hearts together in bonds of love. That distance so kept up has long since, perhaps, hindered you from enjoying the smile and love of your Saviour. It *has* done so; it *ought* to do so. The withholding of His sweet presence from your soul in secret *must* be the result of your distance and your unforgiving spirit towards one you are bound to love. Oh banish it, and live in unity and godly love!

But in what measure is this grace given? "According

to the measure of the gift of Christ." One of the most striking marks of the Deity, in nature and providence, is *adaptation.* So is it in grace. God gives His spiritual blessings *wisely* as well as lovingly. He gives just what the child can bear to receive, so much as He sees that child will be able to use for His glory. He adapts the treasure to the *vessel,* and the vessel to the *treasure* to be put into it. He sees our natural failings, our idiosyncrasies, our delicate bodies, our tender minds, our sensitive disposition. Our whole framework is open before Him, and He gives that which is adapted to each one. If we have small grace, the fault is not *His.* No. " He giveth *more* grace." He may deepen the vessel to receive larger measures of grace. He *will* if we ask Him. He often does by casting it into the furnace of trial. There is sadly too little of His grace in the vessel. He sees it, and is determined that that vessel shall hold more. Sorrow, trial, afflictions, " deeps calling unto deep," all His " waves and billows going over us," these are generally the means He uses. As to ourselves, while we are the subjects of this strange dealing, we seem to be *going back.* But no; we are *advancing.* This is God's way. We advance by going backward, we grow strong by becoming more weak. The vessel is deepening; and just now we shall see more grace in it. It will shine forth before men. That hasty temper will yield, that selfish disposition, those hard thoughts of others. There will be less grasping after this world's vanities, a deeper humility, a kinder spirit, a gentler tone, a readier disposition to condemn ourselves. All this will be. The process may be long. It may take years to produce it. But the man is now a contrast to what he formerly was. Ah, there is more grace! The "vessel" is deepened. There is more of "the treasure" in it now.

And let us remember, if we have little grace the fault is ours, not His. He giveth " grace according to the measure of the gift of Christ." And what is Christ's measure? Love, infinite love. We are not straitened in Him, but in ourselves. When Abram interceded for Sodom, God did not stop *granting*, till Abram stopped *asking*. When Elisha poured the oil in the Shunamite's vessels, the *oil* ceased not till the *vessels* ceased. There was "not a vessel." When Jesus opened His treasures on the mount, and fed the multitude, *His supply* did not stop till *they* ceased in their demand. "As much as *they would*," this was God's measure. So it is now. Christ's measure is infinite. *We* are straitened, not *He*. We draw so little on His ocean fullness, and therefore we have so little to praise Him for. Therefore we see so little of the fullness of Christ to meet our necessities. He is the same now as on the mount of old. If we are hungry, He is all fullness. If we are in a desert place, we have all things in Jesus. He asks us to *sit down* to *rest* even in our "*desert* places," and let Him feed us out of His Almighty resources. God often brings us into a desert place, but it is only that we may learn something of Jesus that we knew not before. Oh these are lessons we have not learned yet with all our learning! They are lessons learned only in the **desert**, only at the feet of Jesus.

"Wherefore He saith, When He ascended up on high, He led captivity captive, and gave gifts unto men. Now that He ascended, what is it but that He also descended first into the lower parts of the earth?" Mark, dear reader, how Christ is our example here. He "*descended first*," before

He "*ascended* up on high." Every gift from on high is made to depend on this: He "descended *first*." So must it be with us. If we would ascend, we must *first* descend. We must go down in ourselves, if we would be spiritually great. We must be nothing if we would be anything in God's sight. We must be humble if we would rise. It is now the order with all the members, as it was with the living Head, we must "descend *first*." Oh to have this spirit deepened within us! Oh to be *descending* here! If we would indeed *ascend*, it must be so. If we would, like our ascending God and Saviour, "give gifts to men," be of any real spiritual blessing to others, we must "descend first." It is the law of nature. The tree whose branches rise *highest* in the air has its roots *deepest* in the earth. The lofty peaks of the Andes have at their base the deepest depths. If we had of old stood on Ebal, the mount of cursing, we could not have crossed over to Gerizim, the mount of blessing, without going down to the bottom of the intervening gorge. So must it be with us. To descend is to rise. To be little is to be great. To be humble is to be a blessing to others.

"He that descended is *the same* also that ascended up far above all heavens." What a comforting word! Though at the right hand of the Father, He is "the same" as when, in lowliness and grace and love, He trod our earth. No word is sweeter to the child of God than this: "the same." Behold Him, all grace and love, jaded and wearied at the well of Sychar! See the dust on His sandals, and the sweat on His brow! Listen to His loving words and earnest tones to a guilty outcast. The thirst is forgotten. The drink of water is lost sight of in the earnestness of His soul to win a sinner's heart. Is He still the same in that glory, where angels and archangels veil their faces before Him? Yes. He who thus descended is "the same," though far above all heavens. Behold Him again in the temple. Hear His words of grace to one whose life was scarred and blotted with sin. How sweet the accents as they fall on the sinner's ear! "Neither do I condemn thee; go and sin no more." Yes, though high in glory, though cherubim and seraphim pant with delight to do Him honor, precious thought, He is still "the same." Mark Him in the house of the Pharisee. See how He throws His shield over another sinner. Hear His word of commending love: "She hath done what she could." Behold His tears at the grave of one whom He loved! See how He weeps over the guilty city, as with words of anguish, He exclaims, " O Jerusalem, Jerusalem, how often would I have gathered thee, as a hen gathereth her chickens under her wings, and ye would not!" Hear His dying prayer, while the taunts of the soldiers, and the yells of the rude rabble were ringing in His ears: "Father, forgive them; for they know not what they do." Yet is He who thus "*descended;*" who thus emptied Himself of His glory, and "made Himself of no reputation," still "the same" Jesus. Time has not changed His love. Sins and shortcomings, failings and provocations have drawn no chill over *His* heart. He is still the same true and trusted Friend and Brother as of old. "The same," though in highest glory; "the same yesterday, to-day, and forever." Yes, and when that world's glory shall dawn upon the soul, when the opened heavens shall disclose to our view the King in His beauty, the eye and the heart of each waiting child of God shall be cheered and gladdened by beholding "that *same* Jesus so coming as He went away." Each one shall hear that voice as of old, whispering to his soul, amid the storm and desolation around, "Good and faithful servant, enter thou into the joy of thy Lord."

But mark the purpose for which He ascended. "He that descended is the same also that ascended up far above all heavens, *that He might fill all things.*" Dear Christian reader, it is not heaven nor the heaven of heavens that can fill thy soul. That poor thirsty spirit of thine can be filled only by One who is "*far above* all heavens." Oh yes, heaven is a poor thing without Jesus! We need One far above the *highest* heavens. Our emptiness can be filled by no angel or archangel, by no harp of gold or crystal sea, or jasper walls, or pearly gates. The soul stretches its wings higher and higher still. The panting spirit feels the poverty of all these. It finds no rest but in soaring. And not till it has found the Saviour, does it find that which "fills" its aching void. When the glories of the highest heavens have passed in review before it, still its language is, "Whom have I in heaven but Thee? and there is none upon earth that I desire in comparison of Thee."

And if Christ has indeed gone up on high for the purpose of "filling all things," what does this imply? A great and glorious truth, that everything in which *He* is not, is unfilled. Yes, reader, if "Christ, the hope of glory," be not in thy soul, with all thy fullness—intellectual fullness, moral fullness, religious fullness—thou art an empty man. If there be in thy heart any affection unshared by Him, it has vanity written upon it with the finger of God. If there be any aim, any plan, any duty, any way of thine whatsoever that does not culminate in His glory, it is all empty, and thou wilt find it so in the end. The handwriting of heaven may be seen on everything which Christ does not "fill:" "Thou art weighed in the balances, and found *wanting*." There is only one thing can give stability, substance, weight, or reality to anything under heaven, or in heaven, and that is Christ. Reader, remember this, and beseech Him to give character and solidity and reality to everything pertaining to thee, by filling it with Himself.

But, before we pass on, let us notice another striking truth contained in this passage. The words rendered "into the *lower parts* of the earth," may be more correctly rendered "into the parts *lower than* the earth," and are placed in antithesis to "far *above all* heavens." Thus no creature can rise to the height to which He has risen, nor descend to the depth to which He has descended. He has gone lower than the earth, and higher than the highest heavens. And why beneath the earth and higher than all heavens? That He might embrace "all things," both in the one and the other. This is God's purpose concerning His dear Son: "that He might gather together in one all things in Christ, both which are *in heaven* and which are *on earth;*" " that at the name of Jesus every knee should bow, *in heaven* and *in earth* and *under the earth*, and that every tongue," not only of men and angels, but of inanimate nature, for everything has a tongue, "should confess that Jesus Christ is Lord, to the glory of God the Father." This, then, is the reason why "He descended *lower than* the earth, and ascended *far above all heavens*," that all things might be gathered within *the embrace* of our Jesus, "that He might *fill* all things." And soon we shall see it. The possession is already "purchased." The inheritance has been redeemed by blood. Soon shall the King of kings claim it as His own. Then shall man reflect His image. The likeness of a "*man*," the man Christ Jesus, shall be seen in everything. The dumb creation shall be blessed in Him. The blade of grass and the opening flower shall reflect His beauty. The trees of the wood shall rejoice and sing. We shall breathe a holier atmosphere, a more genial air. The desert shall blossom as the rose. On the very bells of the horses shall be inscribed " Holiness to the Lord." Yea, " every *pot* in Jerusalem shall be holy to the Lord of hosts." The name of Jesus shall be written on the very forehead of every child of God. Then shall "He *fill* all things." Nature shall know of no vacuum, for all things shall be filled, as now they are empty, with the fullness of Him " in whom all fullness dwells."

And mark God's design in the gifts of the ascended Saviour. "And He gave some, apostles; and some, prophets; and some, evangelists; and some, pastors and teachers; for the perfecting of the saints, for the work of the ministry, for the edifying of the body of Christ; till we all come in the unity of the faith, and of the knowledge of the Son of God, unto a perfect man, unto *the measure of the stature of the fullness of Christ.*" All God's gifts, whether to His Church corporately, or to His people individually, are for this end, to make them like Christ. All the processes of nature, all the actings of Providence, all the discipline of nations, all that passes from day to day, and from generation to generation, in our world, are for this end, that the glory of Christ may be ultimately evolved. Everything in nature, providence, and grace, ever since man fell, has been going on for this end.

And mark what *rest*, what *calmness*, what *stability*, the possession of Christ gives to the soul. "That we henceforth be no more children, *tossed to and fro*, and *carried about by every wind* of doctrine, by the *sleight of men*, and cunning craftiness." The unconverted are constantly compared in the Bible to *chaff,* and the Lord's people to wheat. The chaff has the *shape* and the *likeness* of the wheat, but it has not the *internal substance* (see Psalm i. 4). It is mere profession without substance. Therefore, the *chaff* is " carried away by every wind," while the wheat remains. The chaff is " *tossed* about " like a withered leaf, from one place to another, and no human foresight can perceive where it will be next. All this is because it is *hollow.* It lacks *substance.* The " sleight of men " is a remarkable expression. In the original it signifies " the diceboard," that great instrument of cheating and deception by which so many are ruined. Such is the danger to which every soul is exposed that has not *weight* within it, that has not *Christ.*

And let us mark, in closing, one more striking passage. " But speaking the truth in love, *may grow up* into Him *in all things,* which is the Head, even Christ; from whom the *whole body fitly joined together* and *compacted* by that which *every joint supplieth,* according to the *effectual working* in the *measure of every part,* maketh *increase of the body* unto the edifying of itself in love."

We would ask the reader's careful attention, Bible in hand, to this passage. The figure in the apostle's mind is that of the human body, and conveys the most accurate view of the truth contained in it. The mind, the understanding, the will, are all strengthened and developed from the growth of the body. Thus believers grow, and their growth is the development in them of the Head, even Christ. He becomes strong in them. They "*grow* up into *Him* in all things, which is the *Head.*" Observe how **the apostle from this point** *extends* the figure. All the members of the human body being "*fitly* joined," the shoulder-bone to the shoulder, the hand to the hand, the foot to the foot, become "*compacted*," or joined together by the circulation of the blood, " by that which *every* joint supplieth." The members thus being *set* by the skillful Anatomist, they *adhere* by the internal circulation. Like the picture of the valley of dry bones. Man's spiritual members are all disjointed by sin. God comes into the scene. He, the skillful Anatomist, *sets* the disjointed members, " bone to *his bone*." Thus they are "*fitly* joined together," for everything done by God is "*fitly*" done. Then the Spirit of God, the life-blood of the spiritual body, circulates, and thus the members "*fitly* joined," become "*compacted*" by that *inner circulation*. And that *compacting* depends again upon the healthy action of the heart, sending forth its currents unimpeded through every "joint" of the body. Thus it is that by "that which every joint supplieth" from the " *effectual working in the measure of every part* " the body is increased, and grows up "an holy temple in the Lord."

Reader, see that *you* are not the chaff, having the shape, the form, the profession of the wheat, but without the substance. Oh see that you make no mistake *here!* See that you have *Christ* in you. See that you know Him, love Him, follow Him. See that you can say, " He loved *me* and gave Himself for *me*." See that it is no mere words, no mere scriptural phraseology, no mere profession of your creed, but with reality, with depth, with earnestness, with intensity of truth, you can say, " Lord, Thou knowest all things, *Thou knowest* that I love Thee." " Whom have I in heaven but Thee? and there is none upon earth I desire in comparison of Thee." All religion without this is a sham, a cheat, a hollow mockery, and *odious* in the sight of God.

> Do you love Christ? I ask not if you feel
> The warm excitement of that party zeal
> Which follows on while others lead the way,
> And makes His cause the fashion of the day.
> But do you love Him when His garb is mean;
> Nor shrink to let your fellowship be seen?
> Do you love Jesus, blind and halt and maimed?
> In prison succor Him, nor feel ashamed
> To own Him, though His injured name may be
> A mark for some dark slanderer's obloquy?
> Do you love Jesus in the orphan's claim?
> And bid the widow welcome in His name?
> Say not "When saw we Him?" Each member dear,
> Poor and afflicted, wears His image here;
> And if unvalued or unknown by thee,
> Where can thy union with the body be?
> And if thou thus art to the body dead,
> Where is thy life in Christ, the living Head?
> And if dissevered from the living Vine,
> How canst thou dream that thou hast life divine?
> Sweet is the union true believers feel,
> Into one spirit they have drunk, the seal
> Of God is on their hearts, and thus they see
> In each the features of one family!
> If one is suffering, all the rest are sad;
> If but the least be honored, all are glad.
> The grace of Jesus, which they all partake,
> Flows out in mutual kindness for His sake.
> Here He has left them for awhile to wait
> And represent Him in their suffering state;
> While He, though glorified *as yet* alone,
> Bears the whole Church before His Father's throne.

ISRAEL IN THE WILDERNESS.

Psalm cvii. 1—8.

O give thanks unto the Lord, for *he is* good; for his mercy *endureth* for ever. Let the redeemed of the Lord say *so*, whom he hath redeemed from the hand of the enemy; and gathered them out of the lands, from the east, and from the west, from the north, and from the south. They wandered in the wilderness in a solitary way; they found no city to dwell in. Hungry and thirsty, their soul fainted in them. Then they cried unto the Lord in their trouble, *and* he delivered them out of their distresses. And he led them forth by the right way, that they might go to a city of habitation. Oh that *men* would praise the Lord *for* his goodness, and *for* his wonderful works to the children of men!

The dark background of every picture of God's dealings with man is *mercy*. It is that on which every line is pencilled. Therefore every line is beautiful, and every picture perfect. The soul gazes with wonder and delight on each sketch; and returns, again and again, to gaze with unwearied delight. It is the landscape of the great Artist, every touch of whose hand is perfection, light, and beauty.

So is it here. "O give thanks unto the Lord; for He is good; for *His mercy* endureth forever." This mercy is the first verse of the chapter. Everything that follows is founded on it. It is the dark background. The redemption, the discipline, the care and watchfulness, the love and grace recorded in the chapter, are characters drawn upon this. The blessings of the gospel are built upon the death of Christ, out of which they all flow.

"Let the redeemed of the Lord say so." Yes, it is their hearts that should be filled with gratitude, and their lips with praises. What has not Christ done for us? What is He not to us, day by day, and hour by hour? What will He not be in the countless ages of eternity? Surely *our* lips should be vocal with praise! Only eternity can tell how much we owe to Him. Only when we stand in His presence, and see with unsinning heart and unveiled eyes, shall we know how much He has done for us.

> "Then, Lord, shall we fully know,
> Not till then, how much we owe."

"And gathered them out of the lands, from the east and from the west, from the north and from the south." Yes, He has "gathered" and still gathers His people. It is the Shepherd's voice they hear, as He seeks them, and brings each one home to the fold. He "gathers the lambs in His arms." He gently places them in His bosom. He leads them safely across the desert. He finds them where the shepherd often finds his sheep, in *strange* hiding-places. Some in the thicket, or the deep morass, or the dark jungle; their fleece torn and they bleeding. Thither the good Shepherd bends His steps, stoops down, and gently lifts on His shoulders the bleating wanderer, and carries it home to the fold. Oh, out of what strange hiding-places have God's people been *gathered*, in this cloudy and dark day! And still He is seeking and gathering them, and not one shall be missing. There shall be "a multitude which no man can number, of all nations and kindreds and people and tongues." And the Lamb, who gathered each one in His *grace*, shall lead them in everlasting *love* " to living fountains of waters; and God shall wipe away all tears from their eyes."

"They wandered in the wilderness in a solitary way; they found no city to dwell in." After the Lord has *redeemed* His people they find themselves in the wilderness. From the moment we came to know, to love, to follow Jesus, we felt the world to be a " wilderness," and we but " strangers and pilgrims " here. Now, the pillar of cloud and the pillar of fire are our guide, our light, our all. Now, we live on the manna from heaven, and drink the living waters from the smitten rock.

Nor do we find the world a wilderness only. It is also " *a solitary* way." So long as we lived in Egypt, and on Egypt's plenty, we felt none of this cross, this loneliness, this severance from all earthly attractions. But now we have to walk a lonely path. The world will have none of us. It casts out our name as evil. It rejects and despises the Lord we love and live upon. It calls us narrow-minded, weak, and enthusiastic. Smiles that once greeted us and gladdened our hearts have given way to alien looks and estranged affection. Yes it is " a solitary path," and we feel it is. And yet it is full of sunshine, full of joy, full of gladness, full of peace! We go not back in heart to Egypt. We would not exchange places with theirs for ten thousand worlds! We have *one* Companion and Friend and Brother. He is with us and we are with Him. Oh the path is very bright, and never brighter than in the deepest darkness! We are alone, but *indeed* we are *not* alone. Each one can say in his most lonely hour:—

> "Oh! I know the Hand that is guiding me,
>   Through the shadow to the light;
> And I know that all betiding me
>   Is meted out aright.
> I know that the thorny path I tread
>   Is ruled with a golden line;
> And I know that the darker life's tangled thread,
>   The brighter the rich design.
>
> When faints and fails each wilderness hope,
>   And the lamp of faith burns dim,
> Oh! I know where to find the honey-drop
>   On the bitter chalice brim.
> For I see, though veiled from my mortal sight,
>   God's plan is all complete,
> Though the darkness, at present, be not light,
>   And the bitter be not sweet.
>
> I can wait till the day-spring shall o'erflow
>   The night of pain and care;
> For I know there's a blessing for every woe,
>   A promise for every prayer.
> Yes; I feel that the Hand which is holding me
>   Will ever hold me fast;
> And the strength of the Arm that is folding me
>   Will keep me to the last."

Here "they find no city to dwell in." Their hearts are with the Saviour on His throne. They "*look* for a city which hath *foundations*, whose builder and maker is God." This world has no foundation. It and all that is in it is built on the sand. The storm is at hand which shall rock it to its base. But they, "according to His promise, look for new heavens and a new earth, wherein dwelleth righteousness." Their city has *many* foundations. For it they are waiting. They long for its appearing, and they cry, "Come, Lord Jesus, come quickly." Their citizenship is now in heaven. Their sun is about to rise. Their glory is about to appear. And that morning shall dawn in glory and beauty, a "morning without clouds," never to know a shadow again.

Yet here they have their troubles, their sorrows, their sins. But the Lord is with them. He hears their cry, and delivers them. He fills their mouth with praises. "Hungry and thirsty, their soul fainted in them. Then they cried unto the Lord in their trouble, and He delivered them out of their distresses." Their trials only bring out new themes for praise; their conflicts, more of the Lord's grace to meet them; their sins, more of the value of His precious blood which has put them all away.

"And He led them forth by the *right* way." Yes, though it often seemed to them a *wrong* way, though they were "at their wits' end," though Pharaoh was often behind and the deep sea before, yet was it a "*right* way." Though often they had, while here, to pass through floods and flames, often hungry and thirsty, and having no city to dwell in; often with the heavens over their heads as brass, and their feet bleeding with thorns, yet was it after all a "*right* way." Often that way was through the chambers of death, the heart bleeding and desolate, the mind staggering under its load, and the eye scalded with bitter tears; often all God's waves and billows rolling one after another over their soul; often stooping down and looking into the sepulcher of buried hopes and fond affections; often with the piercing cry bursting from the heart, "My God, my God, why hast Thou forsaken me?" yet it was a "*right* way." Yes, it may be a strange way to us. God may often have to say to us as He said to Israel of old, "Ye have not passed this way heretofore;" yet be sure, tried and tempest-tossed child of God, it is a "*right* way." He is too loving to lead you by any other; He is too wise, as well, to let you lose your crown.

And what is the object of all this? "That they might go to a city of *habitation?*" Yes, to a city of *habitation.* It is the sweet word "home" that sounds in our ears in this verse. There is no city to dwell in here. There is no habitation for the heart in a wilderness. No; "we look for a city." Our home is with Jesus. Till then with joy would we walk a solitary path. It was His when here, and it shall be ours "till He come." Meanwhile, He is "leading us forth by a right way to a city of habitation." Then let us praise Him for His goodness. Let us dwell on His love. Let us lean on His arm. Let us come up out of the wilderness. "Only a few more shadows, and He will come." The morning is near, very near. Oh to be ready, waiting, watching, working for our precious Lord! Let us cast off every work of darkness. Let us put on now more than ever the armor of light. Let us have no cowardly shrinking, no indecision for Christ marking us. Let us "*in* season and *out* of season," too, be *faithful* to Him. The times we live in are solemn. The form of godliness is increasing, but the power of it is fast going out. Compromise of principle, indecision for Christ, half-heartedness for His glory, concession to error, and secret communion of soul with God dying out; these are some of the saddest features of the Christianity of our day, and are rapidly on the increase. Christian, be warned! watch and pray. "Behold, I come as a thief. Blessed is he that watcheth, and keepeth his garments, lest he walk naked, and they see his shame."

Oh abide, abide in Jesus,
  Who for us bare griefs untold,
And Himself, from pain to ease us,
  Suffered pangs a thousand-fold;
'Bide with Him, who still abideth
  When all else shall pass away ;
And, as Judge supreme, presideth
  In that dread and awful day.

All is dying ; hearts are breaking,
  Which to ours were once fast bound ;
And the lips have ceased from speaking,
  Which once uttered such sweet sound.
And the arms are powerless lying,
  Which were our support and stay ;
And the eyes are dim and dying,
  Which once watched us night and day.

Everything we love and cherish
  Hastens onward to the grave ;
Earthly joys and pleasures perish,
  And whate'er the world e'er gave ;
All is fading, all is fleeting,
  Earthly flames must cease to glow ;
Earthly beings cease from being,
  Earthly blossoms cease to blow.

Yet unchanged, while all decayeth,
  Jesus stands upon the dust ;
"Lean on me alone," He sayeth,
  "Hope and love, and firmly trust."
Oh abide, abide in Jesus,
  Who Himself for ever lives,
Who from death eternal frees us,
  Yea, who life eternal gives.

THE GOOD PROFESSION.

1 TIMOTHY vi, 10—16.

For the love of money is the root of all evil; which while some coveted after, they have erred from the faith, and pierced themselves through with many sorrows. But thou, O man of God, flee these things; and follow after righteousness, godliness, faith, love, patience, meekness. Fight the good fight of faith, lay hold on eternal life, whereunto thou art also called, and hast professed a good profession before many witnesses. I give thee charge in the sight of God, who quickeneth all things, and *before* Christ Jesus, who before Pontius Pilate witnessed a good confession, that thou keep *this* commandment without spot, unrebukeable, until the appearing of our Lord Jesus Christ; which in his times he shall show, *who is* the blessed and only Potentate, the King of kings, and Lord of lords; who only hath immortality, dwelling in the light which no man can approach unto; whom no man hath seen, nor can see; to whom *be* honor and power everlasting. Amen.

It may be said, perhaps, without fear of contradiction, that most of the ills humanity is heir to spring from misplaced affection. Looked at in a spiritual point of view, it receives a strong confirmation. God, who should be, in a healthy state of mind and body, the *first* object of man's affection, is *actually* the *last*. Nay, more, in man, as we behold him at present, there is not one throb of affection for God in his heart. There may be for God's *gifts*, but for God *Himself* there is none. Hence we conclude that a great change *must* have come over man. It is the conclusion of intelligent reason, unaided by the light of revelation.

It is only in love to God *Himself* that any soul can find its true resting-place. But man loves anything and everything rather than God. His heart is full of idols. And when he can find none *around* him, he makes an idol of *himself*. Hence the misplaced affection and its natural results, the "piercing through with many sorrows."

This is the first truth brought before us in the passage chosen for consideration. "For *the love of money* is the root of all evil; which while some *coveted after*, they have *erred from the faith*, and *pierced themselves through* with *many sorrows*." Mark it, reader; it is simply *misplaced* affection. It is the *love* of something else than God. And it is immaterial what that something else is. It is not *Christ*, and that is enough. It may be money, or fame, or pleasure, or sin. It matters not what it is. It is something else than Christ. Something that has taken His place in the *heart, which is His;* and whatever it may be, *that* is *idolatry*.

And mark the effects of this misplaced affection. They are two, and named in this passage: error in faith, and sorrow of heart. The *heart* is wrong with God, and everything else becomes wrong. The heart wrong with God, and there inevitably follows error in faith, in doctrine, and in all our view of God's character. There can be no true spiritual vision where the heart is wrong with God. How much error there is abroad in the Church, how much spiritual blindness! How is such a state of things to be remedied? By education, by instruction, by teaching? No. You have no guarantee that, with all its instruction, the heart will not be carried away again into error. To begin thus is to begin at the wrong end. Set the heart right with God. See that *it* be *first* true to Christ. Till then all your teaching is vain, though you may enable the intellect to hold the soundest creed on earth. Set the heart right towards God. See that there be no misplaced affection. This done, you may then graft instruction on the heart and understanding. The heart right with God, then will there be purity of faith, and the soul will be preserved from those "piercings through of sorrow" which are the result of misplaced affection.

"But thou, O man of God, *flee* these things; and *follow after* righteousness, godliness, love, patience, meekness. *Fight* the good fight of faith, *lay hold* on eternal life." Let us notice a very important truth in these words. Two things are brought before us. First, that our Christianity is to be *negative* with regard to evil, "*flee* these things;" secondly, that it is to be *positive* with regard to good, "follow after," "fight," "lay hold." We find these two things continually brought before us in the New Testament, and in the *same order*. We invariably find them, too, *united*. If we are told to "*put off* the old man," we are told in the same place to "*put on* the new man." Many Christians, if they are only *negative* with regard to *evil*, are satisfied. If they do "no harm," they are unconcerned as to whether they are actively doing "good." Christianity is no *negative* principle, contenting itself if it be clear of what is wrong. It is positive. It is *aggressive*. It is a "following after," a "fighting," a "laying hold." And yet how often do we hear the cry, "What harm is there in it?" Suppose there *be* "no harm." Were you placed in this world merely to do no harm? Did your

Lord and Master live in this world doing "no narm?" Did He not go about "doing *good?*" What kind of Christianity is yours if it leads you merely to keep yourself from doing "no harm?" Is it positive? Is it aggressive? Is it telling? Is it "*pressing* toward the mark?" Let the reader look at his Bible, and he will find that the Spirit of God never tells us to "*put off*," without at the same time telling us to "*put on*," showing God's great design that the character of His people's religion should be a positive, aggressive thing. And even if in every hour of the day we could live without any charge of inconsistency being brought against us, we should not be acting up to the mind of God, unless there were upon us the *clear marks* of heaven bearing witness for God. Absence from evil is *not* then the ground we are to take, but the "*putting on* of Christ."

"*Lay hold* on eternal life." Let us not mistake these words. They are not addressed to the unconverted, to lay hold of salvation. The unconverted *are* so addressed in the word of God, but not in these words. They are addressed to one who is already saved. The one who has come to Christ, who has been *brought* nigh by the blood of Jesus through the leading of God's Holy Spirit, is exhorted to *grasp firmly* that Saviour who is *holding* him. It is like the passage, "Work out your own salvation with fear and trembling, for it is *God which worketh in you.*" The one so addressed has got salvation. He has not to GET it. He has only to work it out. It is like a workman; he has been given *the material*, and has now only to make it into a vessel. And yet he cannot even do this. *He seems* to be "working out" that salvation *himself*. But no. It is God that "worketh in him, both to *will* and to *do* of His *good pleasure."* So in the passage under consideration. It is to get a firmer grasp of Him who is holding you. Like the child snatched half exhausted from the destructive waves, grasping firmly the loving parent who has rescued him, and holding him securely. We have a similar truth corresponding with this in St. Peter (2d Epistle i, 5, 10, 11); "And *beside this*, giving all diligence, *add* to your faith virtue." "Wherefore the rather, brethren, give diligence to make your calling and election *sure*. For so an entrance shall be ministered unto you *abundantly* into the everlasting kingdom of our Lord and Saviour Jesus Christ." The early part of the chapter tells us what has been GIVEN to us, and from this to go on *adding*. There is the *entrance* to the kingdom through the finished work of the Lord Jesus. No doing of ours can add to that. But there is the *"abundant* entrance" which depends upon ourselves, upon our increase in faith, and holy walk with God, upon our "pressing towards the mark." So we *have* eternal life, but we are exhorted to "lay hold" on it. Reader, are *you* doing this? It is easy to make the passage plain, to *talk* about it, but oh, *are* we living to God?

The apostle now goes on to speak of the "good profession" professed by Timothy "before many witnesses." There is a great amount of *"profession"* on every side, but it is not *"good."* It is the name without the reality. It is the form without the life and power. It is the sickening malaria of the day in which we live. Still the *profession* is not wrong, it is the absence of *life* from it. It wants only one thing to make it a *"good profession,"* the power of God's Holy Spirit quickening, renewing, energizing it. How is our profession to become the *"good* profession?" The apostle tells us: "I give thee charge in the sight of

God, who *quickeneth* all things." Strange that he should connect this passage with the "profession." But we see the Spirit's reason for it. "God, who 'quickeneth' or 'maketh *alive*' all things." This then is the way to make our profession "good," to bring it to the *living God*. Let us go into His presence, have continued and close dealings with Him. Our profession lacks this. *It* has no life, none. It is a poor dead thing. The life is only in *God*. Let us bring the *vessel* there to be filled. Oh that our profession were quickened and made a more *telling* thing than it is, by being brought more into the presence of a quickening God! We want it, oh how deeply! We never wanted it *so much* as in this day. More secret prayer, more getting out of the crowd into solitude with God, more being alone with Jesus, more living under His eye, more living above the opinion and the smile of men. Ah, reader, this is what we want now! See to it, see to it, reader, that thy profession has something of God's breath in it. See to it, for all the living power, all that is value in God's sight, may long ago have left it, and thou be, *to all appearance*, a withered branch; a branch fit only for the fire. The Lord is at hand. See that thy profession is not the "Laodicean" "to be spued out of His mouth." What is there of God in it, reader? What is there of the taking up of thy cross? What is there that speaks of *heaven* in it in each hour of the day? What that speaks for Jesus among thy servants and family, at thy fireside, in thy business, and in all thy dealings with men? What, reader, what? Oh, far better make *no* profession than one which is a mockery of God. See that when God comes in judgment He finds His own breath in thy profession, something of His own image in thy character.

And how is this "good profession" still more effectually to be maintained? The apostle shows us. Mark it well, reader. "I give thee charge in the sight of God, who quickeneth all things, and *before Christ Jesus,* who before Pontius Pilate (or during the rule of Pontius Pilate) witnessed a good confession." It is by "looking unto Jesus." He is set before us here as the One to whom the believer is continually to look, and whose example he is to follow. The Saviour's good confession on earth is to be before us at all times. Yes; to have a good profession the heart must be brought continually into contact with a quickening God, and the eye of the soul be ever "looking unto Jesus."

And how long is this to continue? "That thou keep this commandment without spot, unrebukeable, *until the appearing of our Lord Jesus Christ.*" Yes, this is the blessed hope which is to cheer and animate and encourage the "good profession." This was the great center round which St. Paul made all his exhortations to revolve. It was ever before him. He led everything up to that. That was his *climax.*

And so it should be ours. Brighter and brighter should the "day star" shine before us. The streaks of morning are over the hills. The Sun is beginning to rise, never again to set. "What manner of persons ought ye to be in all holy conversation and godliness, looking for and hasting unto the coming of the day of God?" How should we now be "keeping the commandment without spot and unrebukeable!" How should we be keeping the word in our hearts and in our lives! How should we so keep it that there be no "spot" upon *it* by our inconsistency of conduct! How should we aim to be "without rebuke," "shining as lights in the world!" Reader, see to it that thy profession is a "good" one, that thy life be a living testimony for Jesus.

"Which *in His times* He shall show, who is the blessed and only Potentate, the King of kings and Lord of lords." Yes, "His time" is at hand. Man has had his times; sin and the world, the flesh and the devil have had their times; but *then* Christ shall have His. Every rule of this world has failed to "show" the truth. Everything has been "shown" but Jesus and His word. For six thousand years the world has witnessed Satan's triumph, and Christ and His truth trampled under foot. But the day is at hand when God shall show His Christ, when truth shall be manifested in righteousness, when "a King shall reign and prosper," "Jesus Christ, the same yesterday, to-day, and forever," the "King of kings and Lord of lords." Oh how different will "His times" be from the times the world has ever yet seen! Reader, be ready. "Let your loins be girt," and your lamps trimmed, and you yourself as one who waits for his Lord. "Blessed is that servant whom his Lord, when He cometh, shall find watching."

> Oh to be over yonder,
> In that land of wonder,
> Where the angel voices mingle and the angel harpers ring;
> To be free from pain and sorrow,
> And the anxious dread to-morrow,
> To rest in light and sunshine in the presence of the King!
>
> Oh to be over yonder!
> My yearning heart grows fonder
> Of looking to the east to see the day-star bring
> Some tidings of the waking,
> The cloudless, pure day breaking.
> My heart is yearning, yearning for the coming of the King.

Oh to be over yonder!
Alas! I sigh and wonder,
Why clings my poor weak heart to any earthly thing?
Each tie of earth must sever,
And pass away forever;
But there's no more separation in the presence of the King.

Oh to be over yonder!
The longing groweth stronger.
When I see the wild doves cleave the air on rapid wing,
I long for their fleet pinions,
To reach my Lord's dominions,
And rest my weary spirit in the presence of the King.

Oh to be over yonder!
In that land of wonder,
Where life and light and sunshine beam fair on everything;
Where the day-beam is unshaded,
As pure as He who made it,
The land of cloudless sunshine, where Jesus is the King.

Oh when shall I be dwelling
Where the angel voices, swelling
In triumphant hallelujahs, make the vaulted heavens ring;
Where the pearly gates are gleaming,
And the morning star is beaming;
Oh when shall I be yonder, in the presence of the King?

Oh when shall I be yonder?
The longing groweth stronger
To join in all the praises the redeemed ones do sing
Within those heavenly places,
Where the angels veil their faces
In awe and adoration, in the presence of the King.

Oh soon, soon I'll be yonder,
All lonely as I wander,
Yearning for the welcome summer, longing for the birds' fleet wing.
The midnight may be dreary,
And the heart be worn and weary,
But there's no more shadow yonder, in the presence of the King.

THE SUPPER CHAMBER.

JOHN xiii, 23—26.

Now there was leaning on Jesus' bosom one of his disciples, whom Jesus loved. Simon Peter therefore beckoned to him, that he should ask who it should be of whom he spake. He then, lying on Jesus' breast, saith unto him, Lord, who is it? Jesus answered, He it is to whom I shall give a sop, when I have dipped *it*. And when he had dipped the sop, he gave *it* to Judas Iscariot, *the son* of Simon.

THE incidents of the supper chamber on the night of our blessed Lord's betrayal are full of spiritual instruction. It is to some of these I would particularly direct the reader's attention in the verses I have selected for consideration.

The Lord's Supper presents to our view the real distinction and difference between the sacrificial system of the Old Testament and the spiritual nature of the present dispensation. In the Old Testament the distinctive feature of the sacrificial system was a remembrance of *sin* once a year. In the Lord's Supper it is "in remembrance of *Me;*" that is, of Him who has put sin away. "In the same night that He was betrayed," when our everlasting salvation was being accomplished, at the same moment, the foulest treachery was going on. Thus it may be that in the midst of our highest privileges there may be the betrayal of Christ. The work of Christ has a double effect;

it pardons the sinner in the court of *heaven*, while *faith* brings that pardon into the court of *conscience*. Two striking events are recorded together, connected with this betrayal, the fall of Judas and the restoration of Peter; and they are recorded *together* in order that we may have warning and encouragement side by side.

These are a few thoughts that will naturally suggest themselves on glancing at this scene in the supper chamber. Let us now direct our attention to the passage we have selected for consideration. "Now there was leaning on Jesus' bosom one of His disciples whom Jesus loved." Mark, reader, when it was that the beloved disciple was leaning on Jesus' bosom. It was when *treason* was going on in the room. The darker things grow outside, the nearer should we draw to Jesus. The more Satan puts forth his power in things around, the closer should we draw to our Beloved.

What a picture of the world was this supper chamber! There were together the Son of God and Satan. There was one, and he a disciple, as far off from Christ as a sinner can possibly be. There was another, and he too a disciple, as near as saint can ever be, nearer even than an angel, "leaning on Jesus' bosom." What opposite things were going on in this chamber at the same moment, Christ and Satan; John and Judas; another, Peter, half way; one *leaning*, another *betraying;* one his whole soul penetrated with the love of Christ; another, his whole heart filled with hatred and destruction. Surely it is a picture of our world, drawn with the pen of the Spirit of God!

But where, in the midst of all this, is the true disciple found? "*Leaning* on Jesus' bosom." The *weight* is laid on the *permanent* resting-place. "Cast thy burden on the

Lord, and He shall sustain thee." The very posture of the disciple shows us the repose of his affections in Christ. What a sweet resting-place for the heart! He who had not where to lay His head presents His *bosom* for us to lean upon. Reader, may this place of *nearness and repose* be *your* place, now that treason is gathering round the person of the Lord and His truth on every side of us.

"Simon Peter therefore beckoned to *him*, that *he should ask* who it should be of whom He spake."

Mark, reader, there were *three* kinds of disciples in this room, corresponding exactly with three in the world now. There was one *very near* to Jesus, with a heart filled with His love; this was John. There was another, a *true* disciple, but *at a distance*, and with the evidences of distance in his character, hesitation, want of confidence, fear; this was Peter. There was another, bearing the *profession* of disciple, but with Satan in his heart; this was Judas. These are the three classes of disciples now in the world, and *there are no others*.

But what use did the beloved disciple make of his *nearness?* He used it *for the brethren's sake*, to ask their questions, to relieve their minds, and to solve their doubts and difficulties. Peter, conspicuous on all occasions for boldness of character, is not generally the *last* to ask a question. In this case he is. As he looked on John in that place of nearness and intimacy, he feels that *he* is the one to ask the Lord *that* question, because *the bosom of Jesus is such a place to ask it from*. Words which must halt with fear and dread *anywhere else*, may flow freely there. "Simon Peter *therefore* beckoned to him." Ah, the *boldest* know how to value the disciple *leaning on Jesus*. It is with us as with Peter here; every degree of distance from the Saviour is a place of proportionate uncertainty in our mind towards Him. There is a fellowship and communion with Jesus which can only be had there, "leaning on His bosom." There are words which a disciple is *permitted* to speak to the Lord, and which he may *need* to speak to Him, and which can be uttered *nowhere else*. And the position of the beloved disciple, in this narrative, betokens the entire absence of all *doubt*. There was no thought in his mind about *personal acceptance* with Christ, not a shadow. It was communion of a much higher order. In Peter there was doubt and uncertainty, characteristic of the *distance* at which he stood. In John there was not a shadow. He was in the place of the Beloved in the Song, reposing on the bosom of Jesus, and exclaiming, "Let *Him* kiss me with the kisses of His mouth." Blessed posture of soul! How few now rise up to it! And yet it is the blessed privilege of *every* child of God.

Mark, dear Christian reader, also, that it was in that posture the Lord gave His "new commandment," His commandment of "*love*" (verses 34, 35). The *circumstances* in which the Lord's words find us affect very much the *manner or degree* in which we receive them. If they come to us reposing on the bosom of Jesus, they will affect our hearts and minds in a manner and to a degree very different from that in which they will affect us if we are in the place of *distance*, like Peter. Contrast the calmness and quietness and quick spiritual perception of John with the restlessness and disquiet of Peter. (See verse 37, and chapter xxi, verse 21, contrasted with John's following *without a command*, in verse 20.) What is so *noiseless* as the love of Christ? What makes the heart so calm and quiet? *Hearts* make *homes*. If it be leaning on Jesus' bosom and drinking in His love, there is its *home*. It knows no higher, not even in *heaven*. This *is* heaven.

Dear Christian reader, if *you* should have to ask the Lord a trying and difficult question, go and lay your head on His bosom first: "He then *lying* on Jesus' breast *saith* unto Him, Lord, WHO is it?" Depend upon it we can *wait* for the answer, whatever it may be, if we are only *resting* in Him, reposing on His bosom. Depend upon it, all our strange prayers and restlessness and disquiet may be charged upon the *distance* we live from *Christ*. Live near to Christ. Let your prayer be, "Nearer and yet nearer, Lord, to Thee." Rest satisfied with no place save the bosom of Jesus, on which you may fully and freely lean your aching head, with every weight that shades your brow or presses upon your heart. Live near, very near, and there may you be found when God sends for you.

> Child of my love, lean hard,
> And let me feel the pressure of thy care.
> I know thy burden, child, I shaped it,
> Poised it in mine own hand, made no proportion
> Of its weight to thine unaided strength.
> For even as I laid it on, I said,
> "I shall be near, and while she leans on me
> This burden shall be mine, not hers;
> So shall I keep my child within the circling arms
> Of mine own love." Here lay it down, nor fear
> To impose it on a shoulder which upholds
> The government of worlds. Yet closer come,
> Thou art not near enough; I would embrace thy care,
> So I might feel my child reposing on my breast.
> Thou lovest me? I know it, doubt not then;
> But loving me, lean hard.

THIRSTING FOR GOD.

Psalm lxiii, 1—8.

O God, thou *art* my God; early will I seek thee; my soul thirsteth for thee, my flesh longeth for thee in a dry and thirsty land, where no water is; to see thy power and thy glory, so *as* I have seen thee in the sanctuary. Because thy loving-kindness *is* better than life, my lips shall praise thee. Thus will I bless thee while I live; I will lift up my hands in thy name. My soul shall be satisfied as *with* marrow and fatness; and my mouth shall praise *thee* with joyful lips; when I remember thee upon my bed, *and* meditate on thee in the *night* watches. Because thou hast been my help, therefore in the shadow of thy wings will I rejoice. My soul followeth hard after thee; thy right hand upholdeth me.

THE believer's resting-place is God Himself. Not in God's gifts, however blessed, but in Himself. And when a cloud comes between his soul and the Saviour, not all the gifts of heaven nor all the treasures of earth can compensate for the clouded light of that Saviour's countenance. He will turn away, even from angels in heaven, and exclaim, with a shadowed brow and a heavy heart, "They have taken away my Lord, and I know not where they have laid Him."

It is with this feeling the psalm we have selected for consideration opens. It is the cry of the soul after God, the living God. Still it is the soul in the enjoyment of His presence, but thirsting for more of it. To know God is to long to know more of Him. The soul is full of joy, and yet thirsts for more. One who had known the Saviour as few know Him, exclaimed after a life of devotedness to His service, "That *I may* know Him."

"O God, Thou art my God." Mark the sweet appropriating word, "*my* God." On this hangs everything else in the chapter. We can say nothing if we are not able to say this. It is as if David would say, "Thou great and almighty Being, the framer of the heavens and the earth, in whose hands the nations are as a drop in the ocean, Thou art *my* God." Oh the joy of being able to say at the opening of every chapter in life, "*My* God!" Oh the blessedness of being able, though as a worm of the dust, yet to look up, and gazing on the ten thousand times ten thousand worlds above, exclaim, "*My* God!" Yes, *mine*, and I am His! Let the chapter now be what it may; let it come freighted with sorrow or laden with joy; let it come in tears of grief or beaming with smiles, I am ready.

"*Early* will I seek Thee." Yes, the soul that can say "*My* God," will seek Him early. The new nature which leads that soul to the personal appropriation of Christ, impels it to seek Him *first* in everything. The *opening* thought in every duty, in every pleasure, will be towards Him whose presence fills it with joy. Other claims will indeed come in, but they will come in *afterwards*. The heart will then fully understand and carry out the Saviour's command, "Seek ye *first* the kingdom of God." God's charge against Christians now is, not that they do *not* seek Him, but that they do not seek Him *first*. Other claims come in between them and the Saviour. Thus the heart is "*divided*," and they are "found faulty" before Him.

"My soul thirsteth for Thee, my flesh longeth for Thee

in a dry and thirsty land, where no water is." Mark, reader, two experiences here which always run side by side; the thirsting after God, and the insufficiency of the world. Do we indeed thirst for Him? then we shall feel deeply that this world is "a dry and thirsty land, where *no* water is." But mark, reader, the converse, which is equally true. Do we *not* feel that this world is a dry place? do we feel at rest in it, or find that it occupies unduly our heart's affections? Then there will be *no* thirsting for God. The two things are inseparable. Oh that we would try our hearts by this test, and learn how we stand *experimentally* towards God! Ah, the man who finds this world even a *tolerable* place, can have no *longing* after Jesus! If he *has* tasted and is *daily tasting* the preciousness of Christ, the world is a *very, very* dry place. Reader, what is it to *you?* What is *Jesus* to you?

But what is this thirsting and longing for? "To see Thy power and Thy glory, so as I have seen Thee in the sanctuary." It is for the sanctuary, for the *presence of God.* Alone with Him it has learned His power and His glory. It has *seen* God. It has heard His whisper. It has gazed upon His smile. It has been filled with His breath. The light of heaven has surrounded it. Oh the glory of God's secret presence! What lessons we learn there! What "glory" fills the soul! What "power," to lift us above the world, and above the trials which press sorely upon us! How unspeakably precious the blood on which we have gazed, and which has again and again given peace to our conscience, when we have been all alone with Him! How He has unveiled His face to us, and cheered us with His sympathy, and strengthened us with His love! How He has whispered, "Peace, be still," in many a storm!

How He has clasped us, fainting and falling, in His arms! How He has wiped away the tears from our eyes! How *near* we have felt Him, so near that we scarcely knew whether we were "in the body, or out of the body!" Yes, we have experienced all this in the sanctuary, time after time. We have seen His "power" and His "glory" there, in ways that *nature* could never show it! And we long for it again. Our "soul thirsteth" for Him, our "flesh longeth" for Him. It is a "dry and thirsty land" we are in, and His sweet presence makes us feel it so. There is only one green spot in the desert, and that is "the sanctuary." We long to see Him, as we have seen Him before; and our cry is, "Turn us again, O Lord God of hosts, cause *Thy* face to shine, and we shall be saved."

"Because Thy loving-kindness is better than life, my lips shall praise Thee. Thus will I bless Thee while I live; I will lift up my hands in Thy name." Mark, reader, the psalmist's estimate of God's love, "better than *life*." Life is *everything* to us. Yet here is something he values more than even his life! O reader, what is Christ to *you*? Can you say sincerely, truly, heartily, "I value my Saviour and His love more than *my own life?*" If you cannot, you are unworthy of Him. If you cannot, you *do not know* Him. If you cannot, suspect your religion. It is not *genuine!* If you cannot, then the only solid, reasonable, intelligent conclusion you can come to is, that you have "neither part nor lot in the matter." O reader, try yourself by this test! See that your religion is *real*. See that it will stand the evil day that is at hand, the shaking of all *hearts*, and of all things in the world. *What* are you? *Whose* are you? Is your religion worth a *straw?* Make no mistake, reader. "What think *you* of Christ?"

But observe, further, the psalmist's estimate of Christ: "I will *lift up my hands in Thy name.*" When Moses' hands were *lifted up*, Israel prevailed; when they fell, Amalek prevailed. Prayer is victory. The neglect of prayer is defeat. "I will lift up my hands in Thy name." In the name of Jesus is victory. The psalmist associates with that name the "lifting up of the hands," or *victory* over all foes. The "lifting up of the hands" is thus not only the expression of *prayer*, but also of *victory*, and that through the "*name.*" He who can look up and say, "*My* God," knows "in whom he has believed." He knows of no uncertainty. There is nothing doubtful in his course. His eye is on Jesus, Jesus only, and *there* all is *victory*. "The name of the Lord is a strong tower; the righteous runneth into it, and is *safe.*"

"My soul shall be satisfied, as with marrow and fatness; and my mouth shall praise Thee with joyful lips; when I remember Thee upon my bed, and meditate on Thee in the night watches." Every remembrance of Christ to the soul of the believer is precious. There is such joy in the thought of Him that it can only be faintly expressed. And yet we must use figures to convey *some* idea of what Christ is to our souls, though all are so poor. The psalmist uses two here to express it, "marrow and fatness." These are the very *life* and *strength* and *value* of the animal. The "fat of fed beasts," "the fat of lambs," these are the figures constantly used in the Old Testament to express what is most precious in God's sight. This is the figure under which Christ is presented to us in this psalm. The recollection of His dear name is so sweet and "satisfying" to the soul; yea, it is "marrow and fatness." It comes to the soul through the corridors of memory, bringing with it fullness of joy to the longing, thirsting spirit.

> "Tongue never spake, ear never heard,
> Nor heart hath e'er conceived,
> A dearer name, a sweeter word,
> Than Jesus, Son of God."

"Because Thou hast been my help, therefore in the shadow of Thy wings will I rejoice." Again, the psalmist's heart goes back to the presence of God as his *home*. The "shadow of Thy wings" refers to the cherubim on the mercy-seat. There was the ark, the mercy-seat; the cherubim with *outstretched wings*, and over all, the shekinah. Here God manifested Himself. And it is to this presence the soul goes back with "rejoicing." "In *Thy presence* is *fullness of joy*." It is the home of the heart. There is but *one* step beyond, and that is into the unvailed glory of His presence, to see "eye to eye and face to face." Another sweet truth is conveyed under this figure, that of protection and safety. "Because Thou hast been my *help*, therefore in the shadow of Thy wings will I rejoice." Christ is said to be as "the *shadow* of a great rock in a weary land." And His weeping lament over Jerusalem was, "How often would I have gathered thee, as a hen gathereth her chickens *under her wings!* and ye would not." Yes, in the presence of Jesus is protection, safety, and fullness of joy. Happy the man who has learned this from *experience*. Reader, have *you ?*

"My soul *followeth hard* after Thee; Thy right hand *upholdeth me*." Mark, reader, whence the psalmist derives his sense of security, from "following hard" after God. All God's people, from the least to the greatest, are "kept by *the power of God* unto salvation." But if, reader, you want to have the sweet *assurance* of this in your own soul, the *realization* that He is indeed holding you up, and will keep you to the end, then " follow *hard* " after God. The finished work of the Lord Jesus has secured your *everlasting* safety; but your "following hard" after God will bring the sweet assurance and joy of it to your soul. The finished work of Jesus has *given* you an "entrance" into the kingdom, but your "*adding* to your faith" will give you an "*abundant* entrance." Oh "*make* your calling and election sure!" "Follow" after Jesus, but "follow *hard*." "*Press* toward the mark." "*Fight* the good fight of faith." "*Lay hold* on eternal life." "*Wrestle* with the principalities and powers" of evil around you. It will be but for a few days longer. Your labor is now nearly over. Your trials and sorrows are now nearly at an end. Your crown is now almost in your grasp. How *near* "the day" is now! "Only a few more shadows, and He will come." Follow Christ. Follow *hard*. Follow in the face of the world, the flesh, and the devil. "Hold that *fast* which thou hast, that no man take thy crown."

No shadows yonder!
  All, all light and song
Each day I wonder,
  And say, How long
Shall time me sunder
  From that dear throng?
No shadows yonder!
  All, all light and song.

No weeping yonder!
  All fled away;
While here I wander
  Each weary day;

And sigh as I ponder
  My long, long stay;
No weeping yonder!
  All, all fled away.

No parting yonder!
  Time and space never
Again shall sunder.
  Hearts cannot sever;
Dearer and fonder
  Hands clasp forever;
No parting yonder!
  Hands, hands clasp forever.

None wanting yonder!
  Bought by the Lamb!
All gathered under
  The ever green palm
Loud as night's thunder
  Ascends the glad psalm,
None wanting yonder
  Bought, bought by the Lamb.

GOD'S ANSWER TO THE SINNER'S QUESTION.

MICAH vi, 6—8.

Wherewith shall I come before the LORD, *and* bow myself before the high God? shall I come before him with burnt-offerings, with calves of a year old? Will the LORD be pleased with thousands of rams, *or* with ten thousands of rivers of oil? shall I give my first-born *for* my transgression, the fruit of my body *for* the sin of my soul? He hath showed thee, O man, what *is* good; and what doth the LORD require of thee, but to do justly, and to love mercy, and to walk humbly with thy God?

THE word of God ever directs the sinner's eye to the finished work of the Lord Jesus for peace. It tells him to look to Jesus, to look *now*, and to behold in that finished work his own eternal salvation, that which has brought him nigh to God. It bids him accept it, and go in peace.

It is not generally, however, that the sinner looks directly to Christ. He takes a *circuitous* path, and goes through a *process*, without which he conceives he cannot attain salvation. Thus, instead of believing the finished work of Jesus for his soul, and rejoicing in it, he makes his salvation a matter of *attainment*. Hence the *circuitous* path. Hence the *long process*. Very often this is not the fault of the sinner so much as the obscure way in which the gospel has been accustomed to be put before him. It has been so hampered by conditions, or the *finished* work of Jesus has been put forward in so *unfinished* a manner as to leave him under the impression that he dare not appropriate it without something of himself, of his good life, or his prayers, or his repentance, to *make* it his.

To tell him that it is *his* without any of these, and simply because he is a *sinner*, that his *sin* is his title to it, and not his *goodness*, and that he has only to receive it and rejoice, is to tell him that which he cannot believe. He prefers working to believing. He cannot take it as a *gift*. He must *earn* it.

The passage we have selected for consideration brings before us the history of such a soul. Let us learn its solemn lessons in the light of God's Holy Spirit.

It will be observed that the first five previous verses are occupied with the testimony of God to Israel. Israel is asked to hear, and to plead with God. God brings before them His redeeming love, His watchful care, and declares to them His righteousness.

One is brought before us as affected by this testimony. He is represented as being awakened up by it to inquire about his own relation to God and acceptance with Him. He exclaims, " Wherewith shall *I* come before the Lord ?" It is a blessed thing when we can get the sinner into any state of *concern* about his soul. The crying sin of the majority of those to whom the testimony of the Lord is continually addressed is indifference. When through the Holy Spirit's teachings we can get man to be concerned, to exclaim, "What must *I* do to be saved ?" "Wherewith shall I come before the Lord ?" the sleep is broken, and there is hope.

And this is the way the Spirit of God does it. He presents the *Word*, and brings it home to the conscience. Concern is awakened. The state of the sinner's soul begins to occupy his thoughts more than it used to do. Again and again he tries to banish it. He cannot. Again and again the mournful cry comes up from his heart, "What must I do?" "Wherewith shall I come before the Lord?"

Now comes the circuitous route the sinner takes, the long process and weariness of soul. All this time Christ has been presented and was presented at the very first awakening. "He *hath showed* thee, O man, what is good," is the Lord's rebuke to him afterwards. The "good" *had been shown* at first, but the soul would not look there, and preferred a way of its own.

Mark the stages through which it passes. They form a climax. "Wherewith shall I come before the Lord, and *bow myself* before the high God?" This is the first stage. There is a sense of the greatness and majesty and holiness of God. The *religious thoughts* of the man are at work, and he seeks to "*bow*" himself. He practices humility. He mortifies the flesh. He says many prayers. Still all is vain. He has not peace. Sin is there. It weighs heavily. All he has done yet has not removed it. Again he cries, "What shall I do?" "Wherewith shall I come?"

Mark the next stage. As the sense of sin increases, so do the man's efforts. He makes greater sacrifices. "Shall I come before Him with *burnt offerings, with calves of a year old?*" These are great things, valuable, precious. So he tries them. More attention to religious duties, longer prayers, alms for charitable purposes, better attendance at church, the observance of fasting and other such-like religious duties. Still there is no peace. The man is ill at ease. The heart is not at rest. Sin is there, and conscience holds it before the man. He cannot get rid of it, turn what way he will. It is the specter in his path, night and day. Again the cry comes up from his perplexed heart, "What must I do?" "Wherewith shall I come?"

Mark the next stage. "Will the Lord be pleased with *thousands of rams*, or with *ten thousands of rivers of oil?*" Sin weighs more heavily, and with it the sinner again increases his efforts. Larger sacrifices, longer prayers, scrupulous attention to religious duties, the poor heart deeply probed to root out all its evil weeds; what a process! Still there is no peace. Conscience is more uneasy than ever. The soul is well-nigh in despair. Agony is reaching the climax. Again it cries out with a mournful and bitter cry, "What must I do?" "Wherewith shall I come?"

Mark the next stage. It is the climax. "Shall I give my *first-born* for my *transgression*, the *fruit of my body* for *the sin* of my soul?" It has tried everything the mind could invent or the heart devise. It has lacerated the flesh and torn the limb. It has been on its bare knees for hours, with head uncovered. It has punished the flesh in every way. It has spent hours, or days, or weeks it may be, in prayer. It has given alms of a prodigious character. It has fasted till the flesh has forsaken the body. Still sin is there. Still conscience holds up the dark picture to view, now darker than ever. The heart is tossed to and fro in a tempest of agony and despair. There is no peace, no, none! All is dreariness and misery. All midnight darkness in the soul. One despairing cry comes up from the heart, under the pressure of which it seems ready to burst, "What *must* I do?" "*Wherewith* shall I come?"

Oh painful process! Oh dreary and desolate route for the sinner to take! And yet it is the history of thousands! How does Satan darken the mind, and lead the soul astray! And what multitudes prefer the path *he* suggests, to the clear, simple testimony of God, "The Lord *hath laid* on Him the iniquity of us all;" "It is finished;" "He that believeth on the Son *hath* everlasting life;" "Go in peace, thy sins *are forgiven* thee;" "He hath showed thee, O man, what is good."

The Spirit of God now *reminds* this soul of something He had before presented to it. There is a *rebuke* implied in the words for its *unbelief.* "He hath showed thee, O man, what is good." Look at that He has shown you long ago. Look at that, and not to your doings, for peace. How long will your soul go mournfully exclaiming, "Who will show me any good?" Look at Jesus, there is good, the very good you need. The word "good" comprises everything to be found in the work and life and character of Christ. It contains within itself *all* that God can give to the soul. Look there, sinner, and see all thy salvation. There is the answer to thy troubled heart and sin-burdened conscience. All is in that "good" thing, the Lord Jesus Christ.

And observe: "He hath *showed* thee." It is not something to *do*, but something *done*, *look* at it. It is not to call forth fresh efforts after salvation from *thee*. It is to *behold* salvation accomplished. Thou art the guilty one bitten by the serpent's sting of sin; "*behold* the Lamb of God, which taketh away the sin of the world." "He hath *showed* thee what is good." It is an object presented to the *eye* of the sinner's soul, to which he is directed to look. And the One thus "*shown*" is to be the *attraction* of the soul ever afterwards. He is to be before the redeemed one as the object of delight, of wonder, love, and praise. "*Looking* unto Jesus," he is to "run with patience the race set before him." The One whom *God* has shown to his soul is to *draw* him onward and upward till he stands before the throne.

Now that Christ is presented to the soul, the creature *may, must* begin to work. "What doth the Lord *require* of thee, but to do justly, and to love mercy, and to walk humbly with thy God?" Mark, reader, in this passage, how the order of the natural man is reversed. The one who is here represented as saying, "Wherewith shall I come before the Lord?" has all his thoughts directed to doing and sacrificing first. God shows him the "good" first, and *then* tells him to do. Thus the order of the natural man is entirely reversed. He is not to work *for* salvation, but *from* it. It is not "work," and you shall see "good." It is "look at the good," and then work. It is not "Go and sin no more," and *then* "Neither will I condemn thee;" it is "Neither *do* I condemn thee," *then*, "Go and sin no more." It does not *mock* the sinner by telling him to work for God while it gives him no *motive* for working. No. It gives him a motive for working, the love of Christ to his own soul in the full and free forgiveness of all his sins, and says, "Now go and work for me." "Go home to thy friends, and tell them how great things God hath done for thee."

But mark what the redeemed one is told to do. First, "do *justly*." *Justice* has reference to a *law*. That law is the law of God, the word of God. This is *now* to be his guide, the great rule by which he is to act in all the relations of life.

Second, "love mercy." And why? Because the Lord has shown *such* mercy to *him*, therefore his heart is to be full of it to every one else. He is to be merciful, as his Father in heaven is merciful. The censure, the unkind construction put upon another's words or deeds, the looking at every one in the worst light instead of the best, all this is to be forever put away. He is to "*love* mercy." And this he will do if he knows anything of himself and what the Lord has done for him.

And lastly, "humble thyself to walk with God" (see margin). Why is this? Because God can only walk with the humble. "The proud He knoweth afar off." And if the Christian be not going down daily in *dust and ashes* at the feet of Christ, God *cannot* walk with him. The simple meaning of the passage is this, put yourself each day, each hour, in such a posture of soul that you may have companionship with God. O reader, are you doing this? What does your daily life say to this? What know *you* of having God as a living, abiding companion? Where is your *holiness*, where your *heavenly* mindedness, where your self-denial, gentleness, patience, forbearance, love? Have these indeed a conspicuous place in your daily life? Oh see to it! Have not the worst of all mockeries, the name of Christianity without the power of it. If conscience tells you that you have it not, *seek* it, *pray* for it, *wrestle* with God for it. Rest not till you bear in your daily life a brighter image of Christ than you have done. "Do justly, love mercy, and walk humbly with thy God." Remember, reader, this is no *optional* thing with you Forget it not, the Lord "*requireth* of thee" to do this. May He find you thus living when He comes!

> Judge not: the workings of His brain
> And of His heart thou canst not see;
> What looks to thy dim eyes a stain,
> In God's pure light may only be
> A scar brought from some well-won field,
> Where thou wouldst only faint and yield.

The look, the air, that frets thy sight,
  May be a token that below
The soul has closed in deadly fight
  With some infernal, fiery foe,
Whose glance would scorch thy smiling grace,
And cast thee shuddering on thy face.

The fall thou darest to despise,
  May be, the angel's slackened hand
Has suffered it, that he may rise,
  And take a firmer, surer stand,
Or, trusting less to earthly things,
May henceforth learn to use his wings.

And judge none lost; but wait and see
  With hopeful pity, not disdain;
The depth of the abyss may be
  The measure of the height of pain
And love and glory that may raise
This soul to God in after-days.

ADELAIDE ANNE PROCTER.

THE WOMEN AT THE SEPULCHER.

Mark xvi, 1—8.

And when the Sabbath was past, Mary Magdalene, and Mary the *mother* of James, and Salome, had bought sweet spices, that they might come and anoint him. And very early in the morning, the first *day* of the week, they came unto the sepulcher at the rising of the sun; and they said among themselves, Who shall roll us away the stone from the door of the sepulcher? (And when they looked, they saw that the stone was rolled away), for it was very great. And entering into the sepulcher, they saw a young man sitting on the right side, clothed in a long white garment; and they were affrighted. And he saith unto them, Be not affrighted; ye seek Jesus of Nazareth, which was crucified; he is risen; he is not here; behold the place where they laid him. But go your way, tell his disciples and Peter that he goeth before you into Galilee; there shall ye see him, as he said unto you. And they went out quickly, and fled from the sepulcher; for they trembled, and were amazed; neither said they anything to any *man;* for they were afraid.

THE circumstances in which Christ is placed ever draws to light the true disciple. The death of Christ brings Joseph of Arimathea on the stage of Divine revelation. But for that, who would ever have heard of him? It was the same great event that drew to light another secret disciple, Nicodemus. But for that, who would have known that his Christianity had so grown since the night on which he went to meet the Saviour? It was the circumstances in which that Saviour was placed that brought them out of obscurity and tested their character. And it was simply because of their connection with Jesus that the Holy Spirit gives them a place and a name in the book of God.

It was so then, it is so now. If there was a true disciple anywhere, the circumstances in which the Saviour was placed drew him to light. In this respect He was indeed the *light* of the world, making manifest everything and every one around Him. It is the same now, for Christ is still here in His members. If there be any reality in our religion, the circumstances in which His people are placed will bring it to light. We shall be found gathering round His members to minister to them for the sake of Jesus. If we do not, then there is no reality in our religion. And it is just as we thus gather round Christ, that we are recorded by the Spirit. We get a living name before the throne.

These are the opening features of this narrative. The women are seen round the person of the Lord Jesus. His circumstances have drawn them to light, and given them an imperishable record in the book of God.

Reader, if you want a name in heaven, you must be *in connection with Jesus*. *He* must draw you to light. You will have no record on high but one of shame, if you are not livingly associated with Jesus.

And how very different are the characters seen around Him here! "Mary *Magdalene*, and Mary the mother of James, and Salome." The differences *morally* are great. The difference of degrees of social rank may be great. The world may think much of these things; and man, on account of these things, may be severed from his fellow-man. But *not* around *Jesus*. There *all* are equal. The Spirit of God takes no note of such distinctions. They are seen around *Jesus*, and that is enough. There is the aristocracy of heaven. There is the blood-royal. The Spirit of God, the great Artist of heaven, draws the picture of these women seen around the person of the Lord Jesus, and hangs it up in the gallery of grace, that we may behold and learn.

What urged them onward at this early hour of the day with their spices? Love, only love. "The love of Christ *constraineth* us." This so filled their hearts that there was no room for another thought. The difficulties were never taken into account. The huge stone at the door of the sepulcher, and how it was to be "rolled away," never entered their minds. Love, only love, urged them onward. Love had, no doubt, kept them awake all the previous night, watching for the dawn, and the moments, we may be sure, were long and tedious. What will not the love of Christ do?

But now the difficulties of the way have to be faced. A formidable one presents itself. "Who shall roll us away the stone from the door of the sepulcher?" There was good ground, too, for this difficulty. They were weak women, and the stone was "great." It was no trifling obstacle. It would have turned any one else back. It would have cooled any other motive than the "love of Christ." Ah! *duties* are ours; *issues* are God's. Let us go onward, and leave the "great stone," to God. The love of Christ burns within us. We are going to see the Saviour. Perish every other thought! Leave *difficulties* with God. "Roll thy way upon the Lord; trust also in Him: and He shall bring it to pass."

So they did. The difficulty, the "*great* stone," deterred them not. The love of Christ was stronger. And God, always true to His promise, was true to their *love*.

"And when they looked, they saw that the stone *was* rolled away; for it was *very great.*"

Christian, go onward. Let the love of Christ be thy motive. And if difficulties arise, as they surely will, even the " very great stone," yet pause not to ask " Who will roll us away the stone ?" Leave *that* to God, and go onward. Thy motto is, and must always be, " Onward."

Not only do they find the *stone* rolled away, but receive the glad tidings of a *living* Saviour. The tomb is empty. The herald of heaven is sitting in triumph amid the trophies of death. What a reward for persevering love! Yes, if we go onward under the constraining influence of the love of Christ, two things will always be the result, we shall find difficulties overcome, and that our " labor has not been in vain in the Lord." Love shall have a plain path, though every step of it must be trod by faith. Love shall have a bright reward, for a living Saviour is before it to fill every niche of the heart with gladness and joy.

Still we are in the body. Sin and infirmity intermingle with everything here. They are " affrighted." That which should have filled them with the highest joy, fills them with fear. The empty grave, the pledge of every blessing to the believer, and the triumph of heaven over death, is too much for the heart. Ah! how much God's truth has to contend with before it can find a *home* in our affections. God comes to our souls with the hand full of blessings, and we shrink and tremble, and hesitate and doubt. We fear to take them.

Still, with all this infirmity and sin, the love of Christ was there, and that shall always be corrected if under a cloud, and shall never go unrewarded. " And he saith unto them, Be not affrighted; ye seek Jesus of Nazareth, which was crucified; He is risen; He is not here; behold the place where they laid Him." This is ever the word of Jesus to the loving yet fearful heart, "Fear not." It was always on His lips to strengthen the drooping and to encourage the weak. And why was this said to these women? We are told the reason: "Ye seek Jesus." To those who seek, "all things shall be added unto them." The word of encouragement to every real, earnest *seeker* of Jesus still is, "Fear not."

"But go your way, tell His disciples and *Peter* that He *goeth before you* into Galilee; there shall ye see Him, *as He said* unto you." Yes, seeker of Jesus, "He goeth before you." "Fear not; it is I; be not afraid." At every bend and turn of your pilgrimage-path you may hear His voice, "Fear not; ye seek Jesus; He goeth before you." Through the flood or across the plain; through the dark valley, or over the mountain-height; in the dark path of sorrow, or in the sunshine of prosperity, "fear not," seeker of Jesus, for "He goeth before you." "All things shall work together for thy good." Thou knowest the voice of the Good Shepherd, who "goeth before thee." Thou shalt see Him, even as "He has said unto thee." Thou shalt see Him, and be like Him. Only press on. "Seek Jesus;" and in every path thou wilt see His footprint. Not one good thing of all that the Lord thy God hath promised shall be lacking.

"But go your way, tell His disciples and Peter that He goeth before you." Mark how Peter is specially mentioned here. Man would have said, yea, Christian man, "He basely denied Thee three times. He cursed and swore, and told lies. He acted the coward's part; leave him to himself." Ah, God is not like man. This was the very reason why he *ought* to be remembered. The man whom the world despises, whom the Church would cast out, the Son of God would send a loving message to. Because *he* would be unthought of by man, the Lord would think of him. Therefore the mention specially of Peter, and lest his heart should be swallowed up of sorrow. Oh, the wondrous grace of God, the love of Jesus! How *unlike* men, even the *best* of men! Yes; "go and tell" that Jesus is risen! Tell it to the poor downcast one, the wanderer, the far-off one, that Jesus is risen. Tell the glad news that "captivity is captive led," that death is conquered, and the grave rifled of its prey, for Jesus is risen! Tell it to every poor perplexed pilgrim, toiling his upward way to Zion, Jesus is risen. Tell it; and let every ear listen to the glad sound of victory over death and the grave. Tell it; and bid every heart leap up with joy. He is risen, and we have risen with Him. He is risen, and has left all our sins in the grave where He lay. "He is risen;" let us rise with Him, in newness of life. "He goeth before" us; let us keep our eye on the Conqueror, and follow in His path. "Let us run with patience the race that is set before us, looking unto Jesus." It may be with fears; it may be with trembling; it may be in "amazement," with all the infirmities of a sinful body cleaving to us; still let us seek. Still let us follow, with our eye fixed on Him; and soon the Conqueror's crown shall be placed on the brow of the faithful servant, and everlasting joy shall be on his head.

> What poor weeping ones were saying
>   Eighteen hundred years ago,
> We, the same weak faith betraying,
>   Say in our sad hours of woe.
> Looking at some trouble lying
>   In the dark and dread unknown,
> We too often ask with sighing,
>   "Who shall roll away the stone?"

Thus with care our spirits crushing,
    When they might from care be free,
And in joyous song outgushing,
    Rise in rapture, Lord, to Thee.
For, before the way was ended,
    Oft we've had with joy to own,
Angels have from heaven descended,
    And have rolled away the stone.

Many a storm-cloud sweeping o'er us
    Never pours on us its rain:
Many a grief we see before us
    Never comes to cause us pain.
Ofttimes in the feared "to-morrow"
    Sunshine comes, the cloud has flown;
Ask not, then, in foolish sorrow,
    "Who shall roll away the stone?"

Burden not thy soul with sadness;
    Make a wiser, better choice;
Drink the wine of life with gladness,
    God doth bid thee, "Man, rejoice."
In to-day's bright sunlight basking,
    Leave to-morrow's cares alone;
Spoil not present joys by asking,
    "Who shall roll away the stone?"

THE BLIND MAN OF BETHSAIDA.

MARK viii, 22—26.

And he cometh to Bethsaida; and they bring a blind man unto him, and besought him to touch him. And he took the blind man by the hand, and led him out of the town; and when he had spit on his eyes, and put his hands upon him, he asked him if he saw aught. And he looked up, and said, I see men as trees, walking. After that, he put *his* hands again upon his eyes, and made him look up: and he was restored, and saw every man clearly. And he sent him away to his house, saying, Neither go into the town, nor tell *it* to any in the town.

IN God's word, blessings and warnings are constantly blended together. We sometimes observe the same thing in the actions of the Lord Jesus Christ. There is no truth we lose sight of more than this, that every ray of life and light and healing from above entails a proportionate measure of responsibility. Grace is sensitive, and if slighted will retire. Familiarity with truth brings with it a conscience less impressible to its voice. A step farther it is *seared*. It is a solemn consideration. There is a day at hand when thousands who now pass among men for Christians will wish they had never heard of Christianity. There is an hour approaching when thousands of professedly religious men would give worlds that they never had had any religion at all.

Let us look, in dependence upon the teaching of God's Holy Spirit, on the solemn lessons connected with the healing of the blind man of Bethsaida.

The Lord Jesus, while performing this miracle, was conveying another lesson. While blessing the blind man with restoration of sight, it was done in such a way as to convey a solemn warning. Bethsaida had been a highly favored place. Many of the Lord's mighty works had been done there. The grace and love of the Redeemer had shone forth there in a wondrous manner. Its privileges had been many and great. But Bethsaida had slighted them. It had not repented.

But though grace had been resisted, and the nation still remained impenitent, the Lord does not cast it off. He visits it again. His arms of mercy are again extended to succor the needy. He heals, but in such a manner that they may see how sensitive grace is, and easily grieved by resistance. He heals, but with the manner and words of a wounded heart, and an indication that now their day of grace was over, and His Spirit was about to be withdrawn. "And He took the blind man by the hand." Though grieved and slighted, that hand was ever ready to be extended at the cry of mercy. None ever came in vain. His ear was ever open, His grace ever full and free. The more needy, the more welcome. He would "in no wise cast out."

But mark the significant action, "He led him out of the town." Bethsaida had forfeited, by slighting His grace, all claim to see the works of the Lord Jesus. His withdrawal had a significant meaning. It spoke of a *distance* which the Lord had now taken with regard to it. It conveyed to Bethsaida exactly what familiarity with truth conveys to us, a withdrawal of the Spirit's operations; a conscience less sensitive and tender; a heart less moved than formerly by the voice of God.

Reader, and especially Christian reader, this is a solemn thing. Oh, if there is one prayer more than another you should ever have on your heart, it is this, that you may be preserved from barren familiarity with truth. "Oh," said one, "there was nothing new in what he said; it was just what we all knew before." Here is the terrible effect of familiarity with truth. It becomes inoperative. And how inoperative? That very familiarity was the withdrawal of the Spirit's operation. He cannot work, for the heart and conscience are untouched. Blessed be God, He never withdraws from the soul in whom He has taken up His abode. But He may be grieved, and withdraw His *operations*, leaving that soul to be "saved, yet so as by fire."

Observe how the Lord confirms this by His conduct. "And when He had spit on his eyes, and put His hands upon him, He asked him if he saw aught." How strangely different is this from the Lord's usual manner of healing! He seemed to doubt His own power! What a process, and what a question to put to the man! Why was all this? Slighted grace is sensitive. The Lord doubted not His power. But while the grace should flow from Him as fully as ever, it should flow as from a wounded spirit. It all spoke to Bethsaida of a withdrawal of grace, and that judgment was at hand. The stream of mercy was flowing to the needy, but with reserve and difficulty.

This action is perfect wisdom, and loses nothing of love. If grace has been slighted, it is only right that if manifested again it should be accompanied with some course of conduct to show it is-grieved.

"And he looked up, and said, I see men as trees walking." What a strange effect of the putting forth of the Lord's power! His work only half done! With what difficulty the healing seemed to come! It was as if in a bosom *all mercy judgment* was *struggling* to check the outflowing stream, because of having been resisted. What a solemn lesson for Bethsaida did all this contain!

"After that He put His hands again upon his eyes, and made him look up; and he was restored, and saw every man clearly." Not till now does the full tide of grace come forth. Not till now is the needy one brought under its power. What a process! Yes, to show the danger of slighting the grace of God! It was *retiring*, and the guilty city would soon lose *every* opportunity and privilege. The action of our Lord in every step here is most significant. He had, in all the fullness of grace, *come* to Bethsaida. But because grace had been slighted He takes the man *out of* the town before He heals him, in order to show Bethsaida that henceforward *they* would have *to seek Him*, and *not He them*.

And mark the closing words of our Lord to the blind man. "And He sent him away to his house, saying, Neither go into the town, nor *tell it to any* in the town." Awful words! The message of grace and mercy receives a *positive prohibition* with regard to Bethsaida. It is neither to be there in the person of the restored one as a witness, nor is the message to be carried there. All this because of slighted grace.

"Ephraim is joined unto idols; let him alone." "Make the heart of this people fat, and make their ears heavy, and shut their eyes; lest they see with their eyes, and hear with their ears, and understand with their heart, and convert, and be healed." "Because I have called, and ye refused; I have stretched out my hand, and no man regarded; but ye have set at nought all my counsel, and would none of my reproof; I also will laugh at your calamity; I will mock when your fear cometh; when your fear cometh as desolation, and your destruction cometh as a whirlwind; when distress and anguish cometh upon you. *Then* shall they call upon me, but I will not answer; they shall seek me early, but they shall not find me." "Woe unto thee, Bethsaida! if thou hadst known, even thou, at least in this thy day, the things that belong unto thy peace! but now they are hid from thine eyes." Yes, privilege brings with it awful responsibility! "To whomsoever much is given, of the same shall much be required." Mark, dear reader, several instances of this, and which are *characteristic* of God's dealings. To the poor sinner who had never before heard of His grace, the Lord Jesus went home and abode with him as his honored guest. Zaccheus and the outcast Samaritans, with whom He abode two days, both speak in glowing terms of the fullness and freeness of God's grace to the lost, and His joy in meeting them. But observe how differently He acts with the disciples going to Emmaus. *There* He had opened their understanding. He had spoken to them out of the Scriptures "the things concerning Himself." This was *privilege* on their part. Therefore when He reached their house, "He made as though He would have gone farther." Theirs was the privilege to know the truth, and therefore theirs was the responsibility to act upon it by asking Him to "abide with them." Much had been given, and now much is expected. If they had not asked, grace would have been slighted, because it would have shown that their hearts, instead of "burning within them," had been uninfluenced by His words. This may throw further light on our Lord's words to the woman of Samaria, "*If thou knewest* the gift of God, and who it is that saith unto thee, Give me to drink, *thou wouldst have asked of Him*, and He would have given thee living water." The knowledge would have been the *privilege*, and to ask would have been acting on the responsibility; otherwise grace would have been slighted. Mark, dear reader, one more remarkable instance in confirmation of this. The prophet Isaiah had had his eyes opened by the Spirit of God, to see his true state as a sinner, and the state of every one around him (see chapter vi, 5—8). The grace of God appears with the live coal from the altar, and cleanses him from sin. Oh, this is privilege, the highest of all! But now mark how "much is expected." There is heard a voice from heaven, saying to him, "Who will go *for us?*" It does not say to the prophet, "Go." It asks, "*Who will go?*" It *expects* the answer proportionate to the grace that has been given: "Lord, here am I; send me." If this had not come, grace would have been slighted, because it would have shown that the cleansing had not been valued. O reader, learn the lesson! Let every privilege carry you to prayer, to beseech God to make you *feel* the awful responsibility that has *accompanied* it. You know much, oh aim to *live up* to what you know! "Much has been given," oh strive earnestly in prayer that you be enabled to give back *much!* Never let truth, by familiarity, become inoperative. This has already drawn a veil between God and the souls of thousands of Christians. There is no *love* of secret prayer. There is no *panting* after God's presence. There is a *dullness* within about heavenly things. There is *a distance, painfully felt and carried about with them,* between their souls and God. There is no calm peace or secret joy within. There was *once,* and the conscience has a painful recollection of it as of a thing that has *gone.* Many a soul is bitterly feeling:—

> "What peaceful hours I once enjoyed!
> How sweet their memory still!
> But they have left an aching void
> The world can never fill."

And what is all this? Oh it is the history of Bethsaida over again! It is grace slighted and in the act of retiring. It is an indication of coming judgment on that soul. "Be watchful, and strengthen the things which remain, that are *ready to die:* for I have not found thy works perfect before God. Remember, therefore, how thou hast received and heard, and hold fast, and *repent.* If, therefore, thou shalt not watch, I will come on thee as a thief, and thou shalt not know what hour I will come upon thee." O reader, and especially *Christian* reader, take warning!

> Mark that long dark line of shadows,
> Stretching far into the past;
> Every day it seems to lengthen;
> Whither does it tend at last?
> Each one added to the hosts
> From the present moment flies;
> These are Time's forgotten ghosts,
> Fleeted opportunities.
>
> Characters of light or darkness
> Gabriel's pen from each requires;
> God records, if man forgets them;
> Numbers each as each expires.
> And the awful spectres all
> In the day of God will rise,
> Witnesses at Heaven's call,
> Fleeted opportunities.

Buried powers of good unmeasured,
  Hardly present did ye seem,
Yet I thought I should have treasured,
  When ye vanished like a dream.
Crushing now my sinful soul,
  All your weight upon it lies;
Jesus' blood must o'er ye roll,
  Fleeted opportunities.

O my soul, no further lengthen
  Wilfully this ghostly train;
Rise, and seek for grace to strengthen,
  Where 'twas never sought in vain.
Lost, this hour but adds another
  To those solemn witnesses;
Every living soul's thy brother,
  Mark thine opportunities.

L. N. R.

LESSONS FROM THE WELL OF SYCHAR.

JOHN iv, 1–42.

When therefore the Lord knew how the Pharisees had heard that Jesus made and baptized more disciples than John (though Jesus himself baptized not, but his disciples), He left Judea, and departed again into Galilee. And he must needs go through Samaria. Then cometh he to a city of Samaria, which is called Sychar, near to the parcel of ground that Jacob gave to his son Joseph. Now Jacob's well was there. Jesus therefore being wearied with *his* journey, sat thus on the well: *and* it was about the sixth hour. There cometh a woman of Samaria to draw water; Jesus saith unto her, Give me to drink. (For his disciples were gone away unto the city to buy meat.) Then saith the woman of Samaria unto him, How is it that thou, being a Jew, askest drink of me, which am a woman of Samaria? for the Jews have no dealings with the Samaritans. Jesus answered and said unto her, If thou knewest the gift of God, and who it is that saith to thee, Give me to drink; thou wouldest have asked of him, and he would have given thee living water. The woman saith unto him, Sir, thou hast nothing to draw with, and the well is deep; from whence then hast thou that living water? Art thou greater than our father Jacob, which gave us the well, and drank thereof himself, and his children, and his cattle? Jesus answered and said unto her, Whosoever drinketh of this water, shall thirst again; but whosoever drinketh of the water that I shall give him, shall never thirst; but the water that I shall give him, shall be in him a well of water springing up into everlasting life. The woman saith unto him, Sir, give me this water, that I thirst not, neither come hither to draw. Jesus saith unto her, Go call thy husband, and come hither. The woman answered and said, I have no husband. Jesus said unto her, Thou hast well said, I have no husband; for thou hast had five husbands, and he whom thou now hast, is not thy husband; in that saidst thou truly. The woman saith unto him, Sir, I perceive that thou art a prophet. Our fathers worshiped in this mountain: and ye say, that in Jerusalem is the place where men ought to worship. Jesus saith unto her, Woman, believe me, the hour cometh, when ye shall neither in this mountain, nor yet at Jerusalem, worship the Father. Ye worship ye know not what; we know what we worship, for salvation is of the Jews. But the hour cometh, and now is, when the true worshipers shall worship the Father in spirit and in truth; for the Father seeketh such to worship him. God *is* a Spirit; and they that worship him, must worship *him* in spirit and in truth. The woman saith unto him, I know that Messias cometh, which is called Christ; when he is come, he will tell us all things. Jesus saith unto her, I that speak unto thee am *he*.

And upon this came his disciples, and marveled that he talked with the woman; yet no man said, What seekest thou? or, Why talkest thou with her? The woman then left her water pot, and went her way into the city, and saith to the men, come, see a man which told me all things that ever I did; is not this the Christ? Then they went out of the city, and came unto him.

In the meanwhile his disciples prayed him, saying, Master, eat. But he said unto them, I have meat to eat that ye know not of. Therefore said the disciples one to another, Hath any man brought him *aught* to eat? Jesus saith unto them, My meat is to do the will of him that sent me, and to finish his work. Say not ye, There are yet four months, and *then* cometh harvest? behold, I say unto you, Lift up your eyes, and look on the field; for they are white already to harvest. And he that reapeth receiveth wages, and gathereth fruit unto life eternal; that both he that soweth, and he that reapeth, may rejoice together. And herein is that saying true, One soweth, and another reapeth. I sent you to reap that whereon ye bestowed no labor; other men labored, and ye are entered into their labors.

And many of the Samaritans of that city believed on him for the saying of the woman, which testified, He told me all that ever I did. So when the Samaritans were come unto him, they besought him that he would tarry with them; and he abode there two days. And many more believed, because of his own word; and said unto the woman, Now we believe, not because of thy saying; for we have heard *him* ourselves, and know that this is indeed the Christ, the Saviour of the world.

One of the most remarkable records in God's word is the Lord's conversation with the woman of Samaria. It is like one of those fine landscapes drawn by some master-hand renowned in history, upon which we gaze with rapture. The longer we gaze, the more we seem to admire.

Fresh beauties unfold themselves one by one, which at first we had not noticed. The picture is perfect.

So it is with the chapter we have selected for consideration. It is one of the most striking in God's word for suggestive thought and fullness of detail. Let us look at some of its instructive features.

We are told at the outset, that Jesus "must needs go through Samaria." The necessity for this was twofold; first, because it lay in His way; secondly, to meet and seek and save this sinner. Some would say the latter was the "needs." I prefer to think it was both. God teaches His *spiritual* lessons through the *natural* arrangements and circumstances of daily life. The age of miracles is past. He speaks through the *natural* His manifold *spiritual* lessons. There is wisdom in this. Our way is often to divorce them, to make the natural something with which He has nothing to do. God would teach us to see Him in everything; to mark His spiritual lessons conveyed through *ordinary* events. The natural is the *shell;* the spiritual, the kernel contained in it. The *necessity* was Samaria, because it lay in His way. The spiritual was to meet the sinner *in that way*.

"There cometh a woman of Samaria to draw water; Jesus saith unto her, Give me to drink." How natural all this seems to be! The Saviour, wearied and jaded, and the woman just, as we would say, "happening" to come and draw water, and He asking for a drink. It was just a simple, common-place remark. And yet out of this little thing the Lord raised a great matter. He built on it the great superstructure of the salvation of this woman's soul. It was an ordinary question, but He took it out of the ordinary, and made it great. He thus shows us how we may turn any of the little things of life into a glorious channel. A word, a conversation, a question or answer, if the soul be only right towards God, how we may turn it so as to glorify Him, and make it a great blessing to others! In our general conversation, in our morning calls, in our leisure hours, how little anxiety there is to do this! How many opportunities are lost! How much time is frittered away! How little anxiousness to turn the *passing remark* into a channel that will prove a blessing to those around, and glorify God!

Mark another truth taught us in the Lord's question. His great desire was to win this sinner's soul. How did He begin? By making Himself a debtor to her. He took the lower place, "Give me to drink." There is no way so effectual to gain the heart as to become a debtor to that heart. The higher the ground on which we place that man, and the lower the ground we take ourselves, the more certain we are to succeed. If you want to draw out that heart, to gain an influence over it, make that man kind to you. Ask, and receive some kindness. He who knew man's heart as none else knew it, knew the way to win it, and said, "Give me to drink." Let us do the same, and we too shall possess the power. First will come surprise, then attention, then interest, then desire, and thus the heart will be won.

The natural man lives in the midst of natural things. All his thoughts being under the influence of what is near and seen, he cannot enter into anything higher. Nevertheless, the things seen and temporal, and which press upon us so closely in every hour of the day, are only the medium through which spiritual realities are cast upon us. When we come to look on all here as shadows, and have our thoughts, desires, and affections directed to the substances which are reflected through them, then is God's work accomplished. This is what God, by His Holy Spirit, is striving to bring us to in everything. "The woman saith unto Him, Sir, Thou hast nothing to draw with, and the well is deep; from whence then hast Thou that living water?" The Lord leads her thoughts up to *the* well of which that was only a shadow, to *the* water of which that was only a dim reflection.

"The woman saith unto Him, Sir, give me this water, that I thirst not, neither come hither to draw." The way in which the Lord was leading this woman is strikingly characteristic of His leadings now. To lead man to see that there is something higher than *present* things which he does not yet possess, but which, *if he possessed*, would satisfy his craving after happiness, and thus to create within a desire for that higher thing, is the history of many a well-trodden path from darkness to light. It was thus the Lord was leading this woman. Her attention was roused. Her mind was interested. Her desires were exercised after *this* water which she felt she had not got. The earthly was lost sight of in a desire after the heavenly. And above all, that desire was expressed to One who alone could grant it. This was a new state of things. It was light breaking in on the soul.

But if her desire was to be granted, it must be by conscience being brought under conviction of sin. The "living water" cannot be poured into an *uncleansed* vessel. The heart must be laid bare before God. The conscience must pass through deep conviction of sin. The natural man must be exposed to view, and we must see ourselves; see ourselves, too, in all our deformity in the very presence of the Searcher of hearts. This was now the ordeal through which this woman had to pass. And yet the way in which the Lord proceeded is striking and instructive. His conduct furnishes us with an example which we would do well to follow. He did not point out her sin first, as we generally do; He first tried to win her by receiving a kindness from her. Next He spoke to her about kind things, about the living water, everlasting life, and His willingness to give it. Thus He approached her. *After* all this was done, He said, "Go, call thy *husband*, and come hither." We have a similar illustration of our Lord's mode of acting on the shore of Tiberias. He was about to reprove Peter for *thrice* denying Him on the cross, by asking him *three* times, "Lovest thou me?" Before doing so, however, he says, "Come and *dine*." Thus by disarming the mind of any unkind motive in the rebuke He was about to administer, He rebuked *effectively*. So with this woman. He first spoke of kind things, and thus *prepared the way* for touching her conscience. Before we can *gain the soul*, we must *win the heart*. Our first approach *must* always be love, by *receiving a kindness*. Then we may proceed to reprove. We generally act the reverse of this, and hence the reason we so seldom succeed. Never begin with the *conscience* till you are quite sure you have *won the heart*.

Another point worthy of notice is, that in touching the conscience, our Lord did not begin by expatiating on the corruption of human nature. He did not dwell on *generalities*. He pointed out *one particular sin*, one clear, unmistakable, admissible sin, one from which the conscience could not shrink. So should it be with us. We should be *definite*. We should abstain from *generalities*. We should fix upon a point in the character. When we have brought the conscience fully under the power of that *one* sin, depend upon it we have done more to lead it in repentance to the feet of Christ, than by weeks of sermonizing.

Another point equally worthy of remark, is the gentle way in which the Lord pointed it out. "He whom thou now hast is not thy husband." That was all He said. He passed on to speak of something else. He did not *dwell* on the woman's sin. He did not *keep dragging it to light*, and *holding it up before her*. He just clearly and pointedly brought it to light, and passed on. How often do we spoil a rebuke by dwelling too long on it! How fond we are of *coming back again* to the same point! Oh how unlike Christ! Thus the flesh begins to resent the exposure, and failure is the result. See how marked this was on other occasions in our Lord's life: "Sin no more, lest a worse thing come unto thee;" "Go, and sin no more;" "Her sins, which are many, are all forgiven." How quickly He passed on after, by a word, bringing the sin to light! Oh that we had the Saviour's mind, and could follow His blessed example!

Mark another point. "Go, call thy husband," says the Saviour. But lest the conscience thus touched should, under a sense of shame, retire from His presence, He adds, "and *come* hither." Yes, if the Lord convinces of sin, there is always an encouraging word along with it. If He exposes us to view, it is not to *drive* us from His presence. It is that we may *come* to Him. We may rest assured that whenever the finger of God stirs the stagnant waters of the soul, there is always a voice accompanying His dealings; "and *come hither.*"

Nor need the poor convicted soul fear a rebuke from the lips of Jesus. If the *honest* confession of sin is made in His presence, "I have no husband," it is not to receive the *censure*, but the *approval*. There was the undisguised, candid *confession of her guilt*, and this with the eye of the Searcher of all hearts upon her. Mark the Lord's answer: "Thou hast *well* said;" "In that saidst thou *truly*." No frown, no censure, no condemnation; none! Only the voice of encouragement to the *honest* confession of guilt, "*well*" and "*truly*" said. Oh how encouraging to the sinner to come to Jesus! How gently, wisely, lovingly, *He* deals with the sensitive soul! Others may deal roughly or harshly; *He* is *all* tenderness and compassion. Try Him, sinner, and prove it for thyself!

Little did the woman think when she looked at the Saviour, and said, "Sir, give me this water," what she was asking for, or how it would be granted. We ask to be made to love Him, and that He would give us the peace of His people, and He answers it by exposing our hearts to view, and making us drink the cup of conscious shame and sorrow. We ask, nay, we *sing* :—

> "Nearer, my God, to Thee,
> Nearer to Thee,
> E'en *though it be a cross*
> That raiseth me;"

And we sing it earnestly, too; and God snatches from our side a loved wife, or husband, or darling child, and lays it beneath the green sod. Or perhaps He sends *ruin* on our prospects, and crosses in our family circle, or lays us for years on a sick-bed. Ah! our prayers are being answered, but we never counted on all *this*. Yet "He led them forth by a *right* way." It is *all* wrong, very wrong, if we look at it by *sight*. But faith can say in the midst of it all, "a *right* way." What! the Red Sea before us and Pharaoh and his hosts behind, *that* a *right* way? Yes, faith answers, "a *right* way." "*Stand still*, and see the salvation of the Lord; for the Egyptians whom ye have seen to-day, ye shall see them again no more forever."

The Saviour now brought her *whole life* before her: "For thou hast had *five* husbands; and he whom thou now hast is not thy husband." She saw she was *discovered*. He had gone back into her history for years, and she felt He knew all. She felt an eye was upon her that was gazing down to the very bottom of her heart. And though for a moment, like Adam in the garden, under a sense of sin, she ran to hide herself behind a tree, and that too a *religious* tree, she saw His love and grace, and that chained her to the spot. "Sir, I perceive that Thou art a prophet. Our fathers worshiped in this mountain." What had this to do with the question of her sin? Nothing. It was just conscience, stung to the quick, rushing to hide itself behind the tree.

Still the Lord Jesus does not lay hold of her conscience, and *drag* it from its hiding-place, as some would do. She saw *Him*. She saw *herself*. That was *enough*. He who had opened the wound would never irritate it by dragging the sin again to light. No. He would now sit at that well to *heal* the wound He had made, to "bind up the *brokenhearted*." He follows her in her conversation, suffering Himself to be *led* on, rather than that *He* should lead her; thus preserving the *gracious manner* with which He had commenced. "Our fathers worshiped in this mountain; and ye say that in Jerusalem is the place where men ought to worship." Her ideas of worship were altogether carnal. Living only in the seen and temporal, she associated it entirely with *place.* Gerizim or Jerusalem, either one or the other it must be in. Our Lord raises it to a *higher level.* He takes it out of the region of things "seen and temporal." He divests it altogether of *place.* "God is a *Spirit;* and they that worship Him must worship Him *in spirit* and in *truth.*" He takes her thought about worship, and raises it up to a spiritual level. It is not in a consecrated place or an unconsecrated, and yet it may be in both. These things have nothing to do with it. It is *spiritual.* Worship is in the *heart.* It is the approximation of the heart to God. "God is a *Spirit;* and they that worship Him must worship Him in *spirit.*" It must be your spirit meeting His Spirit. There must be an *affinity* between your mind and His, or else there can be no *approximation of heart.* And where there is not *this,* be what else there may, it is not worship. It is only hypocrisy, even under its best garb.

"The woman saith unto Him, I know that Messias cometh, which is called Christ; when He is come, He will tell us all things. Jesus saith unto her, I that speak unto thee am He." The woman seems in these words to have gathered up all her doubts and perplexities in this word, "I know that Messias cometh; He will tell us all things." It is as if she would say, "I do not know, I cannot see, I am in darkness and doubt; but I know all will be right then." It is these earnest yet perplexed thoughts of the heart that the Lord Jesus came to *meet;* "I that speak unto thee am He." What longings and expectations, what perplexities intermingled with hope, what light struggling with darkness, are to be found shut up in many a bosom, carried through life with a careworn brow and an aching heart! When shall this mystery be solved? When shall these shadows vanish, and we see the meaning of things? To all these thoughts passing to and fro in every breast the Lord Jesus presents Himself, and says, "I that speak unto thee am He." Look at Him. Rest in Him. Let every thought and every affection *culminate* there. Jesus stands at the door of every sensible heart as its longings and sighings after some fancied good escape it, and says, "I that speak unto thee am He." On the threshold of every earthly hope, every ardent desire, every anticipated pleasure, every bright expectation, every earnest craving of the heart, He stands and whispers as of old, "I that speak unto thee am He."

Yes, poor longing one, Jesus is near thee, and always whispering these words! He is nearer to thee than thou hast the slightest conception of, nearer than thy *nearest* desire, or hope, or sigh, and always with the same words, "I that *speak* unto thee am He." He speaks in every hour and in every duty, in every trial and in every blessing, in every joy and in every sorrow, in the bright sunshine of prosperity and at the graveside of every hope, in the stillness of the dying chamber, or amid shadows of the dark valley: "I that speak unto thee am He."

There are no accidents in God's dealings. Arrangement and order characterize each one. Just at this juncture, when the full blaze of the Sun of righteousness had risen on this woman's soul, we are told *"upon this* came His disciples, and marveled that He talked with the woman." Had they come earlier, they might have interrupted the work. But they came just at the right moment, when the work was finished. Adaptation as to *time* is the mark of

God's dealings. It may be said of all of them as it was here, that just at the *right* moment, neither earlier nor later, "*Upon this* came His disciples." But never till God's work is done. Never till *His purpose* has been fulfilled. To us it may appear an interruption or hindrance. To us it may appear to be cut short when only in the bud. But not so to Him. All is wisely ordered, and His glory fulfilling where we least see it.

Not only so, but there is so much in all God's dealings we cannot understand, so much we have to leave unexplained. So it was here. They "*marveled* that He talked with the woman; yet no man said, *What* seekest thou? or, *Why* talkest thou with her?" They could not explain it. They were content to leave it unexplained. And so must we. In every path there are thousands of things we have to leave unexplained in God's dealings. There they are. We see them; but we have to trust. Yet, behind this vail we may be quite sure there are none but gracious designs, as surely as there was behind the vail of ignorance here. They could not see, they did not know, what great things had been going on at the well between the Saviour and this woman. So with us. Where we cannot see, God asks us to trust; and depend upon it, it is because some gracious purpose is behind it all, something beyond our highest thoughts, something that glorifies Him, and will, when we can *bear* to see it, be a blessing to us. We shall praise Him *then* that we did not see it at the time. The sight would have injured us. "What I do thou knowest not now, but thou shalt know hereafter," is legibly written on all God's mysterious dealings.

"The woman then left her water-pot, and went her way

into the city, and said to the man, Come, see a man, which told me all things that ever I did; is not this the Christ?" The earthly water and water-pot and well, where were they now? Pushed out of view. The living water, this now filled every thought of her mind, every affection of the heart. Not that she was not to care for earthly duties. No; but to put them in the *right place*. The *first* thing in her thoughts when she *came* to the well was the *earthly* water. Now she feels there is something which must come before that, however valuable it may be. *Now* the *first* thing is to go into the city, and say, "Come, see a man." This done, she can come back to the well, and get the water to supply her household. Before, it was the creature's wants first, and then Christ. Now it is Christ first, and then the creature's wants. Things are now in their right place. The Fall has *misplaced* everything. In Christ everything is in order.

"Come, see a man, which *told me all things that ever I did*." She felt she was *known*, and yet loved. Though known so thoroughly, she was yet drawn to Him. Oh the blessing of being known! More than half of our troubles and mistakes come from being only half known. "I am not understood," is the common complaint. What a comfort to have to do with One who *fully* knows us! Such a one is Jesus. And herein we rejoice. It is that which draws us to Him when all else are wounding, or deceiving, or misunderstanding us. Oh to look up into His face, and be able to say with one of old, 'Lord, *Thou knowest* all things.'

And what was the burden of her message? what the secret of her success in drawing men to Christ? It was, "Is not this the *Christ*?" Yes, let Christ be prominent in every message, and success must be, whether the ambassador be a feeble woman, or an ordained clergyman. But if Christ be not in His right place, there *can* be, there *will* be, no blessing from God. Reader, and especially Christian reader, mark it well. Let Christ be prominent in your message and conspicuous in your character, and God will make you a blessing wherever you go.

Reader, you may have heard often from the lips of *others*, as the Samaritans heard it from the lips of this woman, about Christ. But have you, like them, *come* to Jesus, and *proved* Him for yourself? Are *you* able to say to the *ambassador* of Christ what *they* said to *her?* "Now we believe, not because of *thy* saying; for we have heard Him ourselves, and *know* that this is *indeed* the Christ, the Saviour of the world." Are you, reader, able to say *this?* Oh, to hear of Christ and to know much of Christ, is a very different thing from being able to say from the heart, "We have *heard Him ourselves*, and know that this is *indeed* the Christ." Rest satisfied with nothing short of this, reader. Rest not till *you* can say, "This is *indeed* the Christ."

> Oft, e'en with those I love the best,
> A cold constraint will lock the breast,
>   And freeze each glowing word;
> But, Lord, how unrestrained and free
> May flow our thoughts and words to Thee,
>   Opening their inmost hoard!
>
> I own earth's friendships pure and sweet,
> Yet often find them vain to meet
>   My spirit's deeper tone;
> Depressed I seek my friend, and find
> Glad thoughts absorb his eager mind,
>   And speak not out my own.

Not so with Thee, O Friend Divine;
My interests are always Thine,
  And claim Thy kindest heed;
Patient where human love must fail,
Nor wearying of the oft-told tale
  Of sorrow, weakness, need.

Oft when the sense of failure hung
Sad on my heart, too sorely wrung
  By shame, regret, and fear,
Thou'st raised my fainting spirit up,
Placed in my hand Thy love's full cup,
  And whispered words of cheer.

Would I not gladly deeper go
Down paths of weakness and of woe,
  Such fellowship to share?
Sweet friendship of my Saviour God!
Beneath it smiles the weary road,
  With heaven's own beauty fair.

BREAD CAST ON THE WATERS.

ECCLESIASTES xi, 1—2.

Cast thy bread upon the waters; for thou shalt find it after many days. Give a portion to seven, and also to eight; for thou knowest not what evil shall be upon the earth.

The figure on which the passage we have chosen for consideration is founded, is striking and instructive. In many parts of India and Africa, and especially on the Nile, when the rivers overflow their banks, the natives may be seen scattering the rice-seed or the corn on the surface of the waters. When the waters subside, the seed thus scattered becomes deposited in the earth, and from it springs a fruitful harvest. Great care has, of course, to be taken by the agriculturist that he do not miss the opportunity. If the seed be not sown at the time of these overflowings, the opportunity is lost, and with it the harvest. Such, we believe, are the facts of the case, and to which allusion is made in this passage. Bearing this in mind, we shall be better able to understand the instructive truths it contains.

The present time is especially one of seed-sowing. Everything done or said here is a seed. Indeed, our whole life stands in relation to the future as a seed. There is not a word we utter but has an influence. There is not an act, however trifling, that does not leave behind *some* impression, however small. Nay, our very *looks* and *tones of voice* carry an influence with them for good or for evil. However obscure we may be, or however known, we each possess in a greater or less degree this tremendous power. We unhappily, through an habitual disregard of *little* things, come to regard only what we call *great* matters as possessing this influence, forgetting that little and great are only terms and measures of our own contracted horizon. Placed side by side with eternity, viewed in the light of God, there is nothing little. Everything is great. The grain of sand assumes an Alpine importance; and so we shall each of us one day find it. The pebble cast into the deep raises a wave which communicates itself far out of sight. Alas for us if we circumscribe its influence to the few rising circles that come under our own observation! This will be indeed to live under the influence of "things seen and temporal." No; let us not deceive ourselves. The smallest things here are seeds cast into the ground; the thoughts and words and deeds, the looks and tones of voice, the "glass of cold water" given to a thirsty disciple, all are seeds sown. The great harvest is before us. Each one in the wonder-working way of God shall be resuscitated. Each one shall start from the grave of oblivion, and standing before conscience, shall recognize its image, and shall proclaim in unmistakable accents, "Thou art the man." Each one shall fill up the measure of that cup now placed by the Almighty in the hands of every living soul. Memory shall be the light that shall irradiate the dark chamber of oblivion, and bring forth its witnesses. And each one starting into existence shall whisper in the ear of that soul, "Son, remember." It is this that makes life so *solemn*. It is this that invests it with an importance thought has never conceived and tongue never uttered. Yes, the *harvest* is before us; and woe to that soul in that day of reckoning, to whose account the blood of Christ has not been laid!

We often see, *even here*, something of religious retribution. We often see how conscience can drag its buried pictures to light, and scare the soul with shadows of the past. "This is John the Baptist; he is risen from the dead," said the guilty Herod, and trembling like a leaf in the hurricane, he presents us with a faint picture of what that day of reckoning will be to each one. Annihilation would indeed be a priceless boon. But annihilation is the lie of the atheist. It is *scientifically* impossible. Yes, even here, at some bend or turn in man's path, conscience drags to light its victim, and standing before the soul, strikes terror through every fiber of the frame by its voice of thunder, "*Thou* art the man!" What shall the reality be, if the shadow is so dark? What shall the morning of the resurrection be, if the land where all is forgetfulness and oblivion be so startling and terrible? We who know these things may well "*persuade* men." God of love, look down in mercy on every unconverted reader of these lines!

But it is not to this passive influence to which this passage exactly refers, though it is included in it. It is to the direct and conscious service of the Christian laborer. It is to the one who sees the *waves* of opportunity rising before him, and making use of the opportunity, scatters the living seed in sure and certain hope of a glorious harvest. It is addressed to one who is working for the *harvest*, to one who knows that he will not *at present* reap, but who nevertheless sows. It is pre-eminently the action of *faith*. He is one who looks not at the "seen and temporal," but at the "unseen and eternal," knowing that "in due season he shall reap," if he slack not his hand now. From the very figure under which the passage is brought before us, it is a thing altogether in the domain of *faith*.

Let us first look at the figure of "bread" under two different aspects, spiritual and natural. Let us look at it first as the emblem of Christ. We are authorized to do this by our Lord's own words: "I am the living *bread* which came down from heaven; if any man eat of this bread, he shall live forever." Again He says, in allusion to Himself, "Except *a corn of wheat* fall into the ground and die, it abideth alone; but if it die, it bringeth forth much fruit." In accordance with this latter statement of our Lord, we may remark that it contains one of the most scientific truths in nature. Everything around teaches us that death is the bosom out of which all life springs. The vegetable world in every form conveys the same lesson. All the glory of Christ's work springs out of His death; and we ourselves never spiritually live except as we are dying to self. Nay, more; all our services have spiritual life in them just in proportion as we throw death into them. In every form we are taught the same striking lesson. The seed thrown into the ground cannot live till it dies. When it reaches the final point of dissolution, it gives forth the germ of a new life.

But to return to the beautiful figure of "bread," as the emblem of the Lord Jesus Christ. Mark the process through which it passes before it becomes food. It is first a seed. That seed grows. There is first the blade, then the ear, then the full corn in the ear. Then there is the ripening. Then it is cut down and *ground* into flour. Then it is subjected to the fiery process of the oven. All this it has to pass through before it can become food for the body. So with the spiritual "corn of wheat," Christ Jesus. He grew up the "tender plant." He was cut down in God's harvest time. "He was *bruised* for our iniquities." He passed through the furnace of God's wrath on the cross. All this He had to pass through before He could become the food of His people. And what is the command now to every Christian man? "Cast thy bread on the waters." Make *Christ* known. Spread abroad the knowledge of His saving name. Tell of His salvation to the lost and guilty. Tell of the saving virtues of His precious blood. Tell of His love and grace and mercy to the needy ones around. Go, speak of Jesus. Have something to say for Him in every conversation. Write some word about Him in every letter. Miss no opportunity. See how the waves are rolling in at your very feet as you stand on the shore of this heaving, restless world. Speak, work, live for Jesus wherever you go. Cast some seed on every wave that rolls in. Be earnest and wakeful and watchful and vigilant for Him. Let not the wave roll back into the great ocean of neglected opportunities, and *you* have to look back, and say, "The harvest is past, the summer is ended," and no seed has been sown, no fruit gathered, for Jesus.

But mark the important little word, "*thy* bread." Ah, reader, is this Christ *thine*? This is the question. You cannot give to *others* what you have not *yourself*. You cannot cast the living bread on the waters if your own soul has never yet fed on it. You may *do* a great deal and yet do nothing for Christ. You may be religious, *very* religious, conscientiously religious, reader, and yet be a *Christless* soul. Again, I ask earnestly, solemnly, *Is* this Christ *thine?*

Let us now look at the figure in the natural view. "Cast thy bread upon the waters." "My time is my bread," has become a proverb, and illustrates the view we would now take of this word. Our time, our wealth, our talents, our influence, these are the "bread" in this point of view. Cast these upon the waves of opportunity, as they roll in upon your path. Gather up the *leisure* moments, and devote them to something that will tell on eternity, something that will leave "footprints on the sands of time." Look around, and see if you cannot by your presence, or by way of encouragement, influence some cause of God that is perhaps languishing. Look around, and see if some of that wealth you are accumulating year by year cannot be spared for God's cause. Look and see if there be not some gratification you could well deny yourself to do good to some hungry, perishing soul. Look and see if some of that time wasted in idleness, or excess of sleep, cannot be redeemed for God's glory. Look and see if you cannot lend a book to some unconverted friend, or write some word for Christ, or brace yourself up to speak faithfully to some one living in sin, or some Christian living inconsistently, at the risk of being called an enthusiast or bigot, a fanatic or fool. Do not clutch your money as if it were your own. It is *not* yours. It is God's gift, for the use of which you will have shortly to give an account; and yet under the garb of a professing Christian you are hoarding it up in thousands for yourself or your family, and your narrow-hearted soul cannot afford even a tenth for God's glory. Look around, and see the luxuries of your household; see your retinue of servants; see your costliness of dress and furniture, and various residences, and yet, what are you doing for *Christ?* Is He not in prison, and you, though bearing His name, never once visit Him? Is He not naked or sick, or His name cast out as evil, and yet you, proud Levite, pass by on the other side, clutching your gold in one hand, and your lifeless, soulless, godless religion in the other? Oh be honest, and cast away the hypocritical mask you are wearing. Give to the winds your hollow, *worthless* religion, and be a worldling *out-and-out.* If you bear that holy name, bear it *honestly.* Be no hypocrite. Be no wolf in sheep's clothing, doling out a few shillings at a time for God's cause, from the mass of gold you are hoarding up. Up and use your opportunities for God more than you have done. Redeem the time. "Cast thy bread upon the waters." Not the *lame,* the *halt,* the *maimed,* for God's service, but "the *small cattle* of thy burnt offerings." Cast not your *husks* upon the waters, but your *bread,* that which is *food* to *yourself,* that which you feel will be a *sacrifice* to you to part with.

And make haste. Time's sun is fast setting. The Lord is at hand. You have, at most, only a few more days to work for Him. Already his chariot wheels may be heard in the distance. Up and seize the fleeting moments, and the long neglected opportunities. The Lord is at hand. What are *you* doing for Christ? How will *you* meet Him? What account will you be able to give of "your Lord's goods?" What will be the reckoning with you as His steward? See to it, reader; see to it!

But *where* are you to cast the bread? "Upon the *waters.*" If you walk or act by sight instead of by faith, you will never cast it *there*, for it will be washed away, and the bread will be lost. Yet God commands us to throw it on the *waters*. How foolish to human reason! Yes, the lessons of *faith* always are to the natural man. God commands us to cast it *there*, where of all other places it seems *certain* to be lost. "Command the children of Israel that they go forward." What! into the *sea?* Yes. Leave that to God. When you obey, He will make a path through that sea. "Take ye away the stone." What use in doing that? What a foolish command! "By this time he stinketh; for he hath been dead four days already." Mark God's rebuke. "Said *I* not unto thee, that if thou wouldst believe, thou shouldst see the glory of God?" What have you to do with *that?* "Said *I* not unto thee?" "Is not *my word* sufficient?" Yes, "cast thy bread upon the waters," the place of death. Be it so. Let us obey. God's word is sufficient.

But the child of God knows something the carnal mind does not know. While he casts the bread, to all appearance, on the *waters*, he knows that *out of sight, down underneath the surface*, there is *solid ground*. Yes; he *knows* this, though he does not *see* it. "Now faith is the *substance* of things hoped for, the *evidence* of things not seen." The word "substance," here, is derived from two expressive Latin words, *sub* and *stans*. They denote that there is something *standing under*, that under the *surface* there is *solid ground*. The Christian seed-sower knows that "his labor in the Lord is not in vain." He casts his bread on the "waters," but he knows it will sink down into *God's* appointed place, and reappear at the great harvest. He can say, "I know whom I have believed, and am *per-*

suaded that He is able to keep that which I have committed unto Him against that day."

Mark, next, the certain promise, "Thou *shalt* find it." It is an individual promise, and one of certain fulfillment. Nothing done for Christ is lost. Each seed, so trifling in appearance, shall yet reappear. Not singly, as when sown, but with a full *ear of wheat*, to be gathered into the garner. And though it may not be till "after many days," yet it shall bring forth its harvest. We are placed in a *waiting* posture. We "know not the day nor the hour when the Son of man cometh." Faith is to be exercised; we are to work and watch, to wait and pray. "What I say unto you I say unto all, Watch." "Blessed is that servant, whom his Lord when he cometh shall find watching."

Let us now notice the second verse of the passage under consideration. "Give a portion to seven, and also to eight; for thou knowest not what evil shall be upon the earth." Mark, reader, the anticipation of the Spirit of God, with regard to what is coming on the earth. It is "evil," not good. It is everything waxing worse and worse, not growing better. It is "as it was in the days of Noah;" "As it was in the days of Lot, so shall it be at the coming of the Son of man." The Spirit of God has but one testimony throughout the Word, whether He speaks by the mouth of the Lord Jesus, or by that of Solomon. It is "evil" that is coming, though we know not its extent or its character. It is a dark picture the Spirit of God has drawn, everywhere in the word of God, with regard to this world's future. The bright side, however, is beyond, "the morning without clouds."

And what will be the true wisdom of the child of God? To prepare for this coming "evil." How? "Give a portion to seven, and also to eight." Seven, among the Jews, was a perfect number. It was God's *due*, His just and righteous demand. The passage taken simply, means, "Do all to God's glory." Give God what is due to Him, every affection and every desire, every motive and every aim, every gift and every talent. Come not short of God's demands. Be up to the mark in everything with regard to Him. Not only so, but "give a portion to *eight*." See that you fall not short *on this side* of God's demand. Let it rather be given *on the other side*. Let it be hearty service, a joyful sacrifice, an uncompromising devotion, a life wholly given to His glory. Not a stinted one, *barely coming up to* His standard, but a *going beyond the letter* of the command, in a full, hearty, spiritual surrender. Better be on the "eight" side, than under the "seven." Let it be "good measure, pressed down and running over," so that all may see whose you are and whom you serve. This will be the only way to meet the coming evil, and the most blessed way to meet the Lord.

Reader, be wholly the Lord's. Beware of a divided heart. Let your eye and aim be single. Have nothing to do with the trimming policy of professing Christians. Be faithful to your absent Lord, as you would desire to meet His smile when He comes. Be faithful, yea, "faithful unto death."

> Sow with a generous hand;
>   Pause not for toil or pain;
> Weary not through the heat of summer,
>   Weary not through the cold spring rain;
> But wait till the autumn comes,
>   For the sheaves of golden grain.

Scatter the seed, and fear not;
  A table will be spread;
What matter if you are too weary
  To eat your hard-earned bread?
Sow while the earth is broken,
  For the hungry must be fed.

Sow; while the seeds are lying
  In the warm earth's bosom deep,
And your warm tears fall upon it,
  They will stir in their quiet sleep,
And the green blades rise the quicker,
  Perchance, for the tears you weep.

Then sow; for the hours are fleeting,
  And the seed must fall to-day;
And care not what hands shall reap it,
  Or if you shall have passed away
Before the waving corn-fields
  Shall gladden the sunny day.

Sow; and look onward, upward,
  Where the starry light appears;
Where, in spite of the coward's doubting,
  Or your own heart's trembling fears,
You shall reap in joy the harvest
  You have sown to-day in tears.

ADELAIDE ANNE PROCTER.

CONTRASTS.

LUKE vi, 46—49.

And why call ye me Lord, Lord, and do not the things which I say? Whosoever cometh to me, and heareth my sayings, and doeth them, I will show you to whom he is like. He is like a man which built an house, and digged deep, and laid the foundation on a rock; and when the flood arose, the stream beat vehemently upon that house, and could not shake it; for it was founded upon a rock. But he that heareth and doeth not, is like a man that without a foundation built an house upon the earth, against which the stream did beat vehemently, and immediately it fell, and the ruin of that house was great.

THE day in which we live presents many solemn reflections to the Christian mind. It has many startling features with which no previous chapter in the history of our world can furnish a parallel. The reserve of former years is giving way to open utterances. Wickedness, always wicked, has never presented itself in such bold, dark colors. Whether socially, morally, spiritually, or nationally viewed, the lines of things are becoming more distinct and vivid. Events which formerly took years to bring to pass are accomplished now in a few days. Electricity and steam have given their coloring to everything; and the work of a life of half a century is now pressed into a few years. This fever or delirium has its baneful effects. The calm, happy, spiritual tone of the soul is injured by it. The hidden life of God is drawn under the influence of the fitful fever outside, and bids fair to reduce many a living soul to the dead level of formal religion.

One of the most dangerous aspects of the time is a widespread counterfeit religion. Men resting satisfied with the belief that the root of the matter, as they call it, is in the soul, inquire no further. Such a soul can differ nothing *outwardly* from a mere professor. The result is, that seeing no practical difference between the converted man and the one who is only a Christian in name, the latter gets the full benefit of being a child of God. Thus those who have only the root of the matter in them, are, by their conduct, helping on the delusion under which thousands are resting. The real and unreal, the spurious and the genuine, have so closely approximated, that the one is mistaken for the other. It was not *always* so. In the early days of the Church the lines of difference were distinct and clear. *Persecution* scattered the chaff, and left the wheat plainly visible to the world. Persecution was the thing that kept the Church alive. Persecution is the only thing that will do it now. And depend upon it the hour is at hand.

Let us contemplate the distinctive features of the two characters in the remarkable words of our blessed Lord we have selected for consideration. Unconverted but professing Christian reader, pause, and mark the lines of difference. Make no mistake here. Thy soul hangs in the balance. It may be that for years thou hast been sailing under false colors, and yet in ignorance of it. May God break thy slumbers!

There are points of resemblance between these two characters, corresponding exactly with two great classes of Christians around us. They both build houses, and the storm comes to both alike, to test the character of their respective buildings. This house is the dwelling-place in which each one is found till that storm comes. The house, the *visible* to all around, is the common Christianity each one professes. Each building has a heavenly *appearance*. It rises upwards, and to the end points in a heavenly direction. To the *observer* one building is quite as good as the other. There is no difference. The real difference between the two is in that which is *not seen.*

The spiritual application of all this is clear and simple. The real Christian and mere professor has each his house, his Christianity in form. The *form* of godliness characterizes both. They both of them point upwards. The *form* of the one is as good as that of the other. The natural eye sees no difference. The one who " walks by sight, and not by faith," regards the house of the fool as being quite as good as that of the wise man. And so it is. The real difference is in that which the eye sees not, in things "*unseen* and eternal," in the hidden foundation. The mind cannot penetrate beneath the surface to look at realities, because it has not the heaven-bestowed power, the light of God's Holy Spirit.

But there is one striking difference between the two, given to us in the words of our Lord Himself at the very commencement. This difference is *vital*. It explains the issue. It is the key to the solution. In speaking of the *wise* man, He says, " Whosoever *cometh to me*, and *heareth* my sayings, and *doeth* them." These are the three stages of real Christianity. The *opened ear*, and the *power to live to* God, resulting from *coming first of all to Christ*. In the case of the foolish man, the first of these is omitted. The man " hears," it is true, but it is the hearing without power. It is the hearing of the understanding, of the intellect, without the power of the Spirit of God to enable him to act; for he "*doeth not.*" And no wonder. He comes not to *Christ*. The Spirit of God is given to none but those who come first to Him. That soul to whom the Spirit of God gives power to "do," He always *first* leads to Christ. The great lesson taught us in this narrative is the truth conveyed all through God's word, that where the ear has been opened by the Spirit of God to hear, there will be the doing, the "fruits" of Christianity; and that where there are not these fruits, the soul has never *really* come to Christ, and consequently the ear has never been opened. It is a work with which the *Spirit of God* has had nothing to do.

But now let us mark the *leadings* of the Spirit of God, where He really begins His work, and carries it on, contrasted with the operations of the natural heart.

The first evidence of His work is to direct the soul to *hidden* things, to "things unseen and eternal." The very first thought of the wise man is the *hidden Rock*. Before he begins to build, or has a thought about building, his attention is directed to this hidden Rock. This guides every future act of his. For this he gets his tools. For this he digs and labors. For this he works on untiringly. He works not *for* salvation, but *from* it. He works not to gain Christ, but because *having* Christ, he can labor hard. What suggests the thought of building? The hidden Rock. What urges him onward? The hidden Rock. What makes him toil in all weathers, going deeper and deeper down? The hidden Rock. What goal is he aiming at, never resting satisfied till he reaches it? The hidden Rock. This, and only this, makes him spend his money, get tools, labor night and day, braving all weathers and all dangers, counting all drudgery delightful. Well might one of old say, "that I may know Him." "This *one* thing I do, forgetting the things that are behind, and reaching forth to the things that are before, I *press* toward the mark." "The love of Christ constraineth us." "Whom have I in heaven but Thee? and there is none upon earth that I desire in comparison of Thee."

Yes, faith urges love onward. He *knows* the Rock is there before he begins. *Love* makes him toil to reach it. These are the great spiritual principles in the narrative. It is simply faith and love working together.

But mark another truth. His very first act in getting towards this Rock is to dig. He goes *down;* and just in proportion as he goes *down* he gets nearer to that Rock. It is the law of nature, providence, and grace, that we rise by descending. We get nearer to Christ by going down. Every step downward is a step nearer to the Rock. O Christian, remember this! The more deeply you descend, the higher you rise. "He that humbleth himself shall be exalted." May your prayer, even in the midst of your praise, ever be,

> "Rock of ages, cleft for me,
> Let me hide myself in Thee."

So this wise man goes down, and continues to go down. He throws aside all the sand, all the superficial coverings in his way. He is no superficial man. His religion is *deep*. It never rests till it rests on the Rock. That is indeed his resting-place. There, too, he *builds*. And from that Rock he *rises heavenward*. It is no rising in appearance, like the other man. It is a rising from a solid foundation. It is a superstructure based on "things *unseen* and eternal," of which Jesus Christ is "the chief corner-stone." What can shake that house? Not all the storms of earth, however vehemently they may beat. Let the flood do its utmost. Let the surges rise. Let the billows roll. What can they do? The house falls not; nay, it is not even "shaken." Why? it is founded on a Rock, the Rock of ages.

Now mark the contrast. See the acting of the foolish man. He builds too. But what of the Rock? Oh, he cares not for that! He builds on the sand. He knows not of the Rock, or if he knows he cares not. Sand will do for him just as well. He is taken by *appearances*. He cares not for *depth*. He cares not for *hidden* things. *What men think*, is everything with him. What the eye sees, is all that concerns him. To pass well in society, to have a fair name, to wear the *garment* of religion, to have all the *outside* commendable, this is all *he* cares about; this is all the *world* cares about. What cares he about the Rock? "His religion is as good as yours; why should he not be saved as well as you? If he is sincere, it is enough. What a bigot you are to condemn everybody who does not think with *you!* What uncharitableness! Go, and keep your narrow-hearted religion to yourself. We are all going to heaven." People see the *houses*. They see no difference. Judging from appearances, one is as good as the other. They know not the *Rock*. They *know* not, and they *care* not. Their religion is like this man's, all on the *surface*.

And when the storm comes, where is the Christian's confidence? In his *house?* Nay, it is in the *Rock*. It is not in his religion, be what it may. It is in something underneath it all. It is simply in Jesus, only Jesus.

But where is the foolish man's confidence? Gone. It is not in the Rock, for he has none. It is not in his house, for he knows right well it was only built and kept up for appearance. Where is his confidence? It is gone. He has none, no Rock, no house, no shelter from the storm. Exposed he stands, with the howling winds around him, the wild waves beating furiously, and the billows rolling over his head. Where is his shelter? Carried by the destructive current to endless destruction, not a vestige left behind! He laughed at the fool so long building the ark! He despised the honest and sincere, but weak enthusiast digging in the earth! He flattered himself all was right, and that in the end he should be no worse than others. So he lived, and so the Lord found him when He came.

And, reader, mark the Lord's closing words in each case. They indicate something *beyond* what the words themselves express. "They could not *shake* it, for it was founded upon a rock." Not only was there no *fall*, but no *shaking*. It rose triumphantly before the blast, and laughed at all its fury. Mark the other. The *very first breath* of God's voice scattered it to the four winds of heaven, "*immediately* it fell." But more than that, as if telling us of something *immeasurably beyond*, " the *ruin* of that house was *great*."

O God, forbid that I should hide from view the eternity of misery with which they will be enveloped who now live for *appearances* instead of *building on the Rock!* I know not, oh I know not, what sounds of woe will ring in the ears of the lost, and this eternally! Oh, I cannot conceive the multiplicity, the intensity, the variety of the torments of the self-destroyed! Only this I know, that the very *character* of God demands it. This I know, that the *justice*, the *holiness*, the *majesty* of God can demand nothing less. The intelligence with which He has endowed me convinces me that it must be so. The exercise of my reason in the works of His own creation leads to the same conclusion. "Who shall dwell with the devouring fire? who shall dwell with everlasting burnings?"

Sinner, be warned! The time is near. It is a portal once passed the step can *never* be retraced. It is a threshhold over which is written in words of light that all may read, "FOREVER!"

Professing Christian, with a name to live, pause and tremble! Thou hast been, and thy secret heart tells thee so, all along living for *appearances*. Think of what *that* day will be to thee! Think of thy *religious* house, thy *moral* house, thy *fair and beautiful* house being scattered like dust, by the very first breath of God, to the four winds of heaven, and thou a naked soul in the presence of thy Judge! Oh fling to the winds thy hollow, false profession! *Be* a Christian, or, like an *honest* man, renounce the name forever. With such a profession, and yet without the reality, thy hypocrisy is of the basest kind. Thou art a hypocrite whose hypocrisy is loathsome. But *what* must it be in the sight of a holy God! Oh cast it away! Far better the atheist's name or the infidel's badge. This at least is *honest;* but *thine* is the blackest hypocrisy in the sight of God and man. May God in mercy awake thee from thy dreaming and slumber, and bring thee to His feet in dust and ashes!

"To you who are troubled rest with us, when the Lord Jesus shall be revealed from heaven with His mighty angels, in flaming fire taking vengeance on them that *know not* God, and that *obey not* the gospel of our Lord Jesus Christ; who shall be *punished with everlasting destruction* from the presence of the Lord, and from the glory of His power."

Rise; for the day is passing,
  And you lie dreaming on;
The others have buckled their armor,
  And forth to the fight are gone.
A place in the ranks awaits you,
  Each man has some part to play;
The past and the future are nothing
  In the face of the stern to-day.

Rise from your dream of the future,
  Of gaining some hard-fought field,
Of storming some airy fortress,
  Or bidding some giant yield.
Your future has deeds of glory,
  Of honour (God grant it may!)
But your arm will never be stronger,
  Or the need so great as to-day.

Rise; if the past detains you,
  Her sunshine and storms forget;
No chains so unworthy to hold you
  As those of a vain regret.
Sad or bright, she is lifeless ever,
  Cast her phantom arms away,
Nor look back, save to learn the lesson
  Of a nobler strife to-day.

Rise; for the day is passing,
  The sound that you scarcely hear
Is the enemy marching to battle;
  Arise, for the foe is here!
Stay not to sharpen your weapons,
  Or the hour will strike at last,
When, from dreams of a coming battle,
  You may wake to find it past.

                ADELAIDE ANNE PROCTER.

SIMEON IN THE TEMPLE.

Luke ii, 25—35.

And behold, there was a man in Jerusalem, whose name *was* Simeon; and the same man *was* just and devout, waiting for the consolation of Israel; and the Holy Ghost was upon him. And it was revealed unto him by the Holy Ghost, that he should not see death before he had seen the Lord's Christ. And he came by the Spirit into the temple: and when the parents brought in the child Jesus, to do for him after the custom of the law, then took he him up in his arms, and blessed God, and said, Lord, now lettest thou thy servant depart in peace, according to thy word: for mine eyes have seen thy salvation, which thou hast prepared before the face of all people; a light to lighten the Gentiles, and the glory of thy people Israel. And Joseph and his mother marveled at those things which were spoken of him. And Simeon blessed them, and said unto Mary his mother, Behold, this *child* is set for the fall and rising again of many in Israel: and for a sign which shall be spoken against (yea, a sword shall pierce through thy own soul also); that the thoughts of many hearts may be revealed.

The narratives of the New Testament are often condensed pictures of the whole system of true religion. They are so full, so comprehensive, so unique, that in one narrative is sometimes comprised the sum and substance of our spiritual life on earth. The teaching in the epistles of the New Testament is but these narratives *expanded*, the *filling up in detail* of a narrative comprised within a few verses. Take, for instance, the narrative of the birth of Christ related in this chapter. From the seventh verse to the twentieth, we have one of these comprehensive outlines, embracing *in order* the following truths: the humility and rejection of Christ; the revelations from God made only to the wakeful, watchful, vigilant soul; heaven's glory surrounding the name of Jesus; unpreparedness of the heart to receive God's messages, and the need of the Spirit's previous preparation; the means the Spirit uses to prepare that heart, the mention of Jesus; the glad message of the gospel, first, to those who hear it, and secondly, a prophetic announcement of its blessing to all the earth; a *full* gospel, "*Saviour*" from *sin,* "*Christ,*" the sent One of God, and "*Lord,*" reminding us that we are "*not our own,*" but His; the mention of Jesus, the cause of heaven's joy as well as the joy of the Church on earth; *obedience* to Heaven's announcement, and the *experience* of joy in consequence, shown in the shepherds going to see for themselves; the "haste," redeeming the time, not allowing a moment to be lost; and the *publishing abroad* the glad news they had seen and heard, as true ambassadors of Christ. And, we ask, what more do the Epistles of the New Testament teach us? Are not these very truths the outline filled up in detail in the Epistles? The Bible is a wondrous book. Its adaptations, its coincidences, its harmonies, its relations between one passage and another, its differences in describing *the same event,* are so marvelous, so striking, so instructive, so manifestly the finger of God, that after a diligent search of threescore years and ten, we come to feel that we have not touched even the *surface* of its "height and depth, and length and breadth!"

Even the very *arrangement* of the *books* of the Bible shows us how wonderfully our compilers were acting under the guidance of the Spirit of God! Take as an instance the Book of Ecclesiastes being placed *immediately before* the Song of Solomon. Why was this? In the former we have the experience of a soul seeking satisfaction from the world, from something " under the sun." This phrase is mentioned nearly twenty times in that book. The man never rises higher than " under the sun." What is the result? All " under the sun" is under the god of this world. It cannot satisfy man's heart. The heart is too large for anything this world can give. It turns away from all, with the bitter cry, " All is vanity and vexation of spirit:" "Man dieth as the beast;" "I hated labor and all that is under the sun." Mark the Song of Solomon. The soul *there* rises *above the sun.* The portion is *then* too large for the heart. Its joy is full, even to overflowing. But is not the experience of the Ecclesiastes *first in order* with all of us? Do we not try the world first? and not till we are driven do we rise from "*under* the sun" to things *above* the sun; from this poor unsatisfying world to Christ. Is not *the very arrangement of these books the order of the soul?* Is it not reflected *in the very order* of our Lord's own words? " Whosoever drinketh of *this water* shall thirst again, but whosoever drinketh of *the water that I shall give* him shall never thirst." Yes, the very arrangement of its books, the very *order* of its words, whether spoken by Solomon or by the Lord Jesus, are Divine, and are the very arrangement and order in the history of the soul.

Before passing to the subject we have chosen for consideration, let us notice one or two remarkable coincidences in God's word to which we have referred, not for curiosity or speculation, but simply to confirm our observation as to the wondrous fullness of the Book of God. A modern writer, in one of the most instructive and beautiful works of recent times, remarks, that "the circle is the archetype of all forms, physically as well as mathematically. It is the most complete figure, the most stable under violence, the most economical of material; its proportions are the most perfect and harmonious. The universe has apparently been framed according to this type. Nature attains her ends, not in a series of straight lines, but in a series of circles; not in the most direct, but in the most roundabout way. All her objects, organic or inorganic, have a tendency to assume the circular form, and in the attainment of this form consists their highest perfection."* He proceeds to give instances of this in every variety of form, from the vegetable world, from the mineral world, from the seasons of the year, from the heavenly bodies, from the structure of the human frame, and its revolutions and vicissitudes. The word of God itself forms a remarkable instance in " the close similarity between the closing chapter of the Book of Revelation and the commencement of the Book of Genesis. The objects that disappear from view after the fall are once more ushered upon the scene." The Spirit of God starts from one point in that circle, and comes round to that point again. The Book of Genesis begins with paradise, the tree of life, the flowing river, man walking with God. The circle has been traversed, and these reappear at the close of the Revelation, only with increased and intensified glory, no longer a solitary pair, but " a multitude which no man can number." We have another

---

* " Bible Teachings in Nature," by Rev. Hugh Macmillan. London : Macmillan & Co.

coincidence connected with this. Adam, placed in a garden, brings himself and his posterity, by sin, into a moral and spiritual *wilderness.* Christ, the second Adam, comes down, takes his place in the *wilderness,* and leads man up into a *garden,* as we behold him in the close of the Book of Revelation. These are striking examples of "undesigned coincidences."

Mark another. Christ was pre-eminently a practical man. He endorsed His precepts with his own example. In John xvi, 33, He *encourages* His people and *comforts* them. He rests not with mere words, however. In John xvii, He confirms His words by *praying* for them. Nor does He rest with even this. In John xviii, 1, He passes from encouragement and prayer to *suffer* for them. He stands between them and the foe, giving up, finally, His life for them. Mark a similar instance in Matthew ix, 36–38. The first thing we observe is the "*compassion*" of His heart for the multitudes. That compassion rests not in mere feeling, as, alas! it so often does with us. It issues in *exhorting His disciples to pray* for laborers. It did not end with mere exhortation. In Matthew x, 1, He calls His disciples to Him, and *sends them* to do the work for which he had exhorted them to pray. Nor did it end here. In Matthew xi, 1, He sets the seal to his compassion, His exhortation, and His work with *them* by giving *Himself* to the work

Again; the Lord Jesus often accompanied his word by some expressive act corresponding with that word. In John xii, 35, 36, He warns the Jews to "walk in the light," lest that light should be withdrawn from them. This solemn warning is accompanied by a corresponding and expressive act; "These things spake Jesus, and departed, and *did hide Himself from them.*" In John viii, 6, is another instance. The scribes and Pharisees bring the *writing* of the law to condemn the sinner. He writes on the ground with His finger, to show that He was the *writer* of that law. In Luke xxiv, 38, is a similarly expressive act, "He made as though He would have gone farther." The word had been spoken; and where that is the case, it ought to be followed by exercise of heart. So it was here. *They* were constrained, and prayed Him to abide with them. This was the *fruit* of the word.

Another remarkable lesson in the narratives of our Lord is one we should all do well to lay to heart. Before He rebuked or reproved, He always strove to *win* the heart. In John xxi, 12, is an instance. He was about to reprove Peter for his third denial of Him, but He first says, "Come and *dine.*" Thus preparing the way for the reproof by disarming the mind of any unkindness in doing so. In Luke viii, 24, 25, He rebukes "the winds and the waves," *before* reproving the disciples for their little faith. In John iv, before He convicts the woman of sin, He speaks of happy things to her soul, the living water, His willingness to give it, and His readiness to receive a kindness at her hands, even a drink of water. Thus the way was prepared.

Again; we often perceive in one chapter, in its several narratives, the leading features, expressed *in order*, of the present dispensation. Mark this in Luke xix. From the first verse to the tenth, we have God's *grace* shown to the *lost*. From the twelfth verse to the twenty-sixth, we have that which follows on the receiving of grace, *responsibility*. In the twenty-seventh verse, we have the next stage, *judg-*

ment. From the twenty-ninth verse to the fortieth, we have the last stage, *glory*.

I have trespassed thus far on the reader's attention with these few undesigned coincidences which have come under my own observation, to confirm my previous statement. Not merely for this, however, but to stimulate to prayerful meditation and deeper research into God's word. Let me now return to the subject I have selected for consideration, in which we shall find a further confirmation of these remarks.

One feature in particular to which we would call the reader's attention is a most important one, and presents itself at the very outset of this narrative, that where man is brought into living association with the Lord Jesus, there the Spirit of God is prominently introduced in connection with every step of his way. Mark it here. Simeon "waited for the consolation of Israel, for 'the *Holy Ghost was upon him.*'" He was to *see* Christ, and through Christ to have his soul so filled with joy as to desire to depart. But who is the author of all this? "It was *revealed to him by the Holy Ghost.*" Again; Simeon is led into the temple, into that place where God reveals Himself, into God's presence. But who leads him? nature? accident? No: "he came *by the Spirit* into the temple."

Oh how clearly God, in his word, sets honor upon the Holy Spirit and upon His work! And yet see how sadly little He is honored in the general preaching and religious literature of the day! After hearing some of the otherwise most excellent preaching, and reading the most excellent works, we might almost be inclined to think that the preachers and writers "had never so much as heard whether there was any Holy Ghost!" Man's efforts, man's preaching, man's writing, *man* is made so much of, and the Holy Ghost so little! No wonder if God doth "blow upon it," and it comes to nought! This is a day when *man* is made much of, and *God* very little. This is a day in which the human intellect is *all but* deified, and the Holy Ghost *degraded*. Reader, depend upon it, if you want to be blessed, if you want God to honor your work, you must honor God's Holy Spirit. Depend upon it, if you make not very much of *Him*, God will make very little of *you* and *your work*.

Mark the three features of this man, under the dominion of the Holy Ghost, "just," " devout," and " waiting" for Christ. And God would have us clearly understand the source of all this; because " the Holy Ghost was upon him." Mark it, reader, well, how everything good in this man's character is traced to *one* cause, and only one, because " the Holy Ghost was upon him." Oh, solemn rebuke to the professing Church in this day of declension and apostasy!

And when the Spirit of God teaches man, what a contrast to the religious teaching of the day! In nothing is it seen more remarkably than in connection with death. Books are written, and sermons are preached, the burden of both being " preparation for death." This is all the blindness and ignorance of poor fallen nature. The Spirit of God does not set *death* before us, but *Christ*. Death is " the last *enemy*." And, strange to say, the enemy is continually put before the sinner, instead of Him who has gotten the victory over the enemy! Mark it here, how different is the Spirit's teaching. He reveals that Christ shall be seen *before* death. Death is *eclipsed* by Him who shines gloriously *between*, the Lord Jesus. The Spirit's preparation for death is to put One between for the eye to rest upon, till we stand in the presence of God; and that One is Jesus, the Resurrection and the Life. Mark this further in the narrative of the transfiguration. What saith our Lord? "There be some standing here that shall not taste of death till they see the Kingdom of God." He placed *between His people and death* the kingdom, the glory, the gladdening beams of the resurrection morning! Yes, whether in the day of life or in the hour of death, the Spirit of God sets before us only *one* object, Christ.

And, reader, learn from this narrative of Simeon what the Spirit would teach you, that you must see Christ *before* death. Oh to see Christ for the first time *after death*, this indeed will be terrible! The soul must see Christ *on this side*, or the meeting will be intolerable. Those who see Him not *here*, can only see Him in judgment. Reader, have you yet seen Him? I warn you, "it had been good for you that you had never been born," to see Him for the first time after you have passed the agonies and throes of a dying hour; or worse than all, after the conscience has been lulled into a false security, and has passed into eternity with a *lie* in its right hand! The Lord's Supper can do you no good. A clergyman's prayers can do you no good. It is all mockery if your own heart has not seen Christ, to believe in Him, to cling to Him, and to lie down to die only in Him!

And where does the Spirit of God always lead the soul after He shows him Christ? Just where He led Simeon, "into the temple," into the presence of God. "My soul thirsteth for Thee; my flesh longeth for Thee, in a dry and thirsty land, where no water is." "My soul thirsteth for God, for the living God; when shall I come and appear before God?" "One thing have I desired of the Lord, that will I *seek* after, that I may *dwell* in the house of the Lord all the days of my life.' "Master, it is *good for us to be here:* let us *build* three tabernacles." "I have a desire to depart, and to be *with Christ;* which is far better."

And when the Spirit of God *leads* a man, Christ always *meets* that man. " Thou *meetest* him that rejoiceth; those that remember Thee in Thy ways." There is no *accident* in that man's life. "*All* things work together for good to them that love God." And the Spirit of God so leads them that every promise of God is fulfilled to them. So it was with Simeon. The Spirit led him just where the promise of God would be fulfilled to him. It was *apparently* accidental. It was through second causes, perhaps. But accidents and second causes are the robe in which God shrouds Himself. He puts on these, and through them *fulfills every promise* to His child. " Every one shall receive of Thy words." So Simeon found it. So all God's people find it. And there is not *one* of God's people now in glory, nay, is there one *on earth*, but can endorse the words of the great lawgiver of Israel, "Not *one* good thing of all that the Lord our God hath promised us hath failed?'

And when the Spirit of God leads a man, it is always to meet *Christ*. It may be to fulfill His promises to the soul, either temporally or spiritually, but it is to see Christ in them. Like Simeon, he may be led into the temple to worship, but it is to meet Christ there. There was the sacrifice, the altar, the vail, the incense, the ark, and the mercy-seat, but oh, what were all these in comparison of Christ to aged Simeon! He seems to say to us, "Painted baubles all, rites, rituals, ceremonies, churches, symbols, creeds, vestments, incense, stoles, chasubles, perish *all*, now that I see *Jesus!*" "Lord, now lettest Thou Thy servant depart in peace." The word is an allusion to those holding offices of state. They cannot leave when they please. They cannot leave till they get the discharge from their sovereign. So Simeon seems to say, "Now, Lord, I am ready. I am satisfied. Give me my discharge. I can go now in *peace*. I want no more. Yet I would not have my will, but Thine. I am ready, willing, yea, will rejoice; but my discharge is in Thy hands. I leave it all where I have left all other things, yes, *all* with Jesus."

> I left it all with Jesus
>   Long ago;
> All my sin I brought Him,
>   And my woe.
> When by faith I saw Him
>   On the tree,
> Heard His small, still whisper,
>   "'Tis for thee;"
> From my heart the burden
>   Rolled away;
>   Happy day!
>
> I leave it all with Jesus,
>   For He knows
> How to steal the bitter
>   From life's woes;
> How to gild the tear-drop
>   With His smile,
> Make the desert garden
>   Bloom awhile:
> When my weakness leaneth
>   On His might,
>   All seems light.
>
> I leave it all with Jesus
>   Day by day;
> Faith can firmly trust Him,
>   Come what may.

Hope has dropped her anchor,
  Found her rest
In the calm, sure haven
  Of His breast.
Love esteems it heaven
  To abide
  At His side.

Oh! leave it all with Jesus,
  Drooping soul!
Tell not *half* thy story,
  But the whole.
Worlds on worlds are hanging
  On His hand,
Life and death are waiting
  His command;
Yet, His tender bosom
  Makes *thee* room;
  Oh, come home! *

Yes, with Christ *pressed to the heart*, there must be "peace." We can then gaze on the swelling flood, and exclaim, "Lord, let me go." But, reader, it must be an *individual* pressing of Christ to the heart, if you are to have peace. *None* without this. None, reader, none. The river of death, without this, will *indeed* look dark and terrible. It does to thee, unconverted one, and no wonder! Without Christ, except in form and profession, and this profession only adding weight to thy condemnation, how could it be otherwise? Without Christ in thy heart, then without God, without peace, without hope, without heaven! How could it be otherwise? "It were good for thee hadst thou never been born." Oh glorious thought, annihilation! But no; this cannot be. Reason, science, philosophy, common sense, all proclaim with united voice, "It is not *possible!*" O reader, hast thou this Christ?

* Ellen W. Willis.

Art thou, like aged Simeon, *pressing* Him to thy heart of hearts? What is *Christ* to thee? What?

And mark the words, "according to Thy word." It shows us God's faithfulness. "He is faithful that promised." Every child of God will, sooner or later, feel that in everything God has been "according to His word." Yes, heaven and earth may pass away, but not one promise of God to His child shall ever fail. We shall each look back on life's journey, and exclaim, "He hath done all things well." Each wave that rises on the shore of everlasting glory shall bear with it the songs of countless hosts, "He hath done all things well." And as the tide rises higher and higher, each heart and each lip shall take up the song from a multitude which no man can number, and repeat the echo, "He hath done all things well." "Blessing, and honor, and glory, and power, be unto Him that sitteth upon the throne, and to the Lamb forever and ever."

And notice the closing words of this inspired hymn: "Which Thou hast *prepared* before the face of all people; a *light* to lighten the Gentiles, and the glory of Thy people Israel." Yes, Christ is *our* "light" and *our* "glory." To poor, down-trodden, outcast Israel, He will shortly be the "glory" too. "They shall look upon Him whom they have pierced." He is, indeed and in truth, the "King of the Jews." They who now call Him a "crucified impostor," shall own Him as their Lord, and He shall be their eternal "glory."

And let us remember that all this is "prepared." A "prepared" Christ, a "prepared" heaven. We are, at present, stones in the quarry of Lebanon. Noiselessly, but surely, the Spirit of God is building the spiritual temple, taking each stone out of the dark quarry, and hewing, shaping, polishing it for the courts of the Lord. All is "preparation" work now. Oh what will the temple be? What will the meeting be? What will the grand reunion of all the scattered members be? What the melody of the golden harps? What the sweetness of the new song? What the jasper walls, and the golden gates, and the glassy sea, and the genial air, and the songs of triumph? What the beauty, the joy, what the glory of *that* hour? Reader, shall *you* be there? Oh remember the word of the Lord, "There shall *in nowise* enter into it anything that defileth." Have you still the defilement of unwashed guilt, unforgiven sin? You *cannot* enter there. See to it, for "the time is at hand." On that morning of joy to some, but morning of terror and wrath to others, one cry will ring through the vaults of heaven, and be heard at the remotest bounds of earth, "He that is unjust, let him be unjust still: and he which is filthy, let him be filthy still: and he that is righteous, let him be righteous still: and he that is holy, let him be holy still."

Christian reader, remember the leadings of the Spirit of God here, "waiting" for Christ, taking of the things of Christ, and revealing them to the soul, being "led" into God's presence, pressing Christ to the heart, and rejoicing in Him, and a readiness to depart and be with Christ. May this be thy path from day to day, thy history till the Lord comes. May He find thee in it. The hour is at hand. Before thine eye follows these lines, He may be here. Oh may the deep, unspoken language of thy heart be, "Come, Lord Jesus!" See that the eye be daily fixed on Jesus, and thy heart true to Him! See that in thy conduct from day to day there is a silent but certain witness for God! See that whether your path be bright or dark, whether one of sorrow or of joy, you are resting wholly on Jesus, and praise Him for everything that makes you lean on Him.

> My God, I thank Thee, who hast made
>   The earth so bright,
> So full of splendor and of joy,
>   Beauty, and light;
> So many glorious things are here,
>   Noble and right!
>
> I thank Thee, too, that Thou hast made
>   Joy to abound;
> So many gentle thoughts and deeds
>   Circling us round,
> That in the darkest spot of earth
>   Some love is found.
>
> I thank Thee more that all our joy
>   Is touched with pain;
> That shadows fall on brightest hours,
>   That thorns remain,
> So that earth's bliss may be our guide,
>   And not our chain.
>
> For Thou, who knowest, Lord, how soon
>   Our weak heart clings,
> Hast given us joys, tender and true,
>   Yet all with wings;
> So that we see, gleaming on high,
>   Diviner things!
>
> I thank Thee, Lord, that Thou hast kept
>   The best in store;
> We have enough, yet not too much
>   To long for more,
> A yearning for a deeper peace,
>   Not known before.
>
> I thank Thee, Lord, that here our souls,
>   Though amply blest,
> Can never find, although they seek,
>   A perfect rest,
> Nor ever shall, until they lean
>   On Jesus' breast!   ADELAIDE ANNE PROCTER.

PARTING WORDS.

JOHN xiv, 1—21.

Let not your heart be troubled: ye believe in God, believe also in me. In my Father's house are many mansions: if *it were* not *so*, I would have told you. I go to prepare a place for you. And if I go and prepare a place for you, I will come again and receive you unto myself; that where I am, *there* ye may be also. And whither I go ye know, and the way ye know. Thomas saith unto him, Lord, we know not whither thou goest; and how can we know the way? Jesus saith unto him, I am the way, and the truth, and the life: no man cometh unto the Father, but by me. If ye had known me, ye should have known my Father also: and from henceforth ye know him, and have seen him. Philip saith unto him, Lord, shew us the Father, and it sufficeth us. Jesus saith unto him, Have I been so long time with you, and yet hast thou not known me, Philip? he that hath seen me, hath seen the Father; and how sayest thou *then*, Shew us the Father? Believest thou not I am in the Father, and the Father in me? the words that I speak unto you, I speak not of myself: but the Father, that dwelleth in me, he doeth the works. Believe me that I *am* in the Father, and the Father in me: or else believe me for the very works' sake. Verily, verily, I say unto you, He that believeth on me, the works that I do shall he do also; and greater *works* than these shall he do; because I go unto my Father. And whatsoever ye shall ask in my name, that will I do, that the Father may be glorified in the Son. If ye shall ask anything in my name, I will do *it*.

If ye love me, keep my commandments: and I will pray the Father, and he shall give you another Comforter, that he may abide with you forever; *even* the Spirit of truth; whom the world cannot receive, because it seeth him not, neither knoweth him: but ye know him; for he dwelleth with you, and shall be in you. I will not leave you comfortless: I will come to you. Yet a little while, and the world seeth me no more; but ye see me: because I live, ye shall live also. At that day ye shall know that I *am* in my Father, and ye in me, and I in you. He that hath my commandments, and keepeth them, he it is that loveth me: and he that loveth me, shall be loved of my Father, and I will love him, and will manifest myself to him.

How solemn are the parting words of one we love! Our heart's affections have learned to twine themselves, like the trembling ivy, round the departing one, and we feel as if the rending tendrils would be plucked from their roots, and wither beneath the blast. With some such feelings did the little band of disciples listen to the words of their loving Saviour, as they fell upon their ears, "Now I go my way to Him that sent me" (John xvi, 4—7).

And was it really so, that the One who had loved them as none else could love was going to leave them? Can that indeed be the way of Infinite love, to leave the sheep in the wilderness, over whom it had wept, and watched, and prayed? Yes; mark the words, "I go *my way*." It was *His* way. It was no accident, no unforeseen occurrence, no strange or capricious step. It was the way of deepest love to "go." Ah! then as now the disciple must walk by faith. To *sight*, it was all wrong. To faith, it was all *well*. It was *God's* way.

And why had He not told them this before? "Sufficient for the day is the evil thereof." God would have His children all joy. He kept all sorrow from them till the last moment. Not till *absolutely necessary* would He have one drop to fall on the soul. He loved them too well to cause a needless tear. "These things *I said not unto you at the beginning.*" Never till the needed moment, the *right* moment, will He speak that which will grieve us. And then it will be only to open behind the dark cloud a rock we have not seen as yet, that shall fill the soul with deeper streams of joy than ever. *We* look only at this *cloud.* He looks at what is *behind,* the deeper joy for the soul, and says, " Nevertheless I tell you the truth." Hard and bitter as you may think it. Strange as it may seem to you to be told that it is " *My* way," " I tell you the truth; it is *expedient for you* that I go away." What! *expedient* for me! This dark cloud, this cutting sorrow, this crushing disappointment, this bleeding heart—expedient! Yes; " *Nevertheless* I tell you the truth; it is expedient for you." You know my love. I never deceived you yet. *Trust* me. now. You cannot *see.* Walk by faith. Remember who it is that speaks to you—your own tried, precious Saviour, the One whom you love, who is everything to you. " *I* tell you the truth; it is expedient for you." Ah reader, child of sorrow, trust that precious Saviour! In every wave that breaks over thy frail bark, hear His voice whispering to thy soul, " *My* way." " I tell you the truth; it is *expedient for you."*

And what was the fault of the disciples here? Just what is always our fault in sorrow. " *None of you asketh me,* Whither goest Thou *?* " You nurse your sorrow. You weep and mourn. The heart goes heavily. You do not come and *ask me* about it. You are trying to bear it yourself. You cannot. It will crush you. Why are you *silent* to me? Come, and look in my face. Come, and lay that burden on my arm. Come, and cast that sorrow on my heart. O poor weary-working, burdened one, come and speak to me about thy sorrows! Is not my arm strong? Is not my love deep? Is not my grace sufficient? Such were some of the Saviour's last loving words to His sorrowing ones on earth.

Let us notice a few more in the chapter we have chosen for consideration. How sweetly it opens! It is the old familiar word of Jesus, "Fear not;" "let not your heart be troubled." Ah, it is always the first word in every chapter that opens upon us from *His* hand, whether of sorrow or joy! It encourages us. Now we can go forward. Come what may—whether His words be dark and heavy, or bright with heaven's own light, still "all must be well." We have at the very outset the sweet and familiar word of One whom we know and love, whom we have tried and found faithful: "Let not your heart be troubled."

The Saviour was about to leave them. The thought of His departure filled the hearts of His disciples with sorrow; and He says to them, "Let not your heart be troubled." He counts upon that departure being a sorrow to their hearts. He counts upon their love to Him in His absence. He cheers them with the blessed assurance that He will come again. Just as when a loved one leaving our fireside for some distant land, yearns fondly over the treasures he is leaving behind, and counts on their continued love to him in his absence, and his last words are, "I shall soon come back again." So with our precious Saviour. "I will see you again, and your heart shall rejoice." "Ye believe in God, believe also in me." You see God in all His works; you believe in Him, that He is living, and guiding, and ordering all, so believe in me. You are certain about God, be the same with regard to me.

And now He tells them that all the time He is away He will be living for them, and engaged in a great and glorious work. "I go to *prepare* a place for you." This was to be His occupation from the moment He left. What wondrous love, to give us this sweet assurance that every hour of His absence would only be the exercise of His heart for them! This was to be the explanation of His absence.

This they were to think of in the loneliness of the way. And then it tells of His grace to our souls! Sinners though we are, and as such anything should do for us, yet even *heaven* has to be "prepared." One whom we love is on his way home. How the heart provides the best and the richest for the expected guest! How the day of arrival is looked forward to! and no time, or trouble, or expense seems enough to lay out in preparation. So it is with Jesus toward us. We are on our way home. What a rich and glorious preparation is going on to welcome us! Nothing is too great or good. Even heaven itself must be made as glorious as only *His* love can make it, for so great a guest as sinners like ourselves! Surely this is love like *His*—love that no heart can compass, no thought can express!

And mark the cluster of blessings which crowd around. "I will come again"—not as a king, not as a ruler, not as a visitor, though all this will be true—but to "receive you unto *myself*." The thought of His *coming* is joy to our souls; but oh, when it is associated with the thought that it is to receive *us*, to clasp *us* to His bosom, to have *us* always in His presence, never again to leave *us*, nor *we* to leave Him—this is fullness of joy!

And what poor worms of the dust we are! How unworthy of Him or His love! Though He had "been so long time" with the disciples, yet Thomas and Philip knew Him not. How like ourselves! How long may He be with us, and how little we may know Him! And yet our ignorance and sin only draw out further revelations of His love. He makes the blind and ignorant confession we make an opportunity of revealing Himself. "I am the way, the truth, and the life." Mark the significance of these words. You wish to go to some distant town. The *way* to it is at your own door. The way to *any* place always lies at every man's own door. Just so Christ is "the way." He is at our very door. He says to us, "Walk on me:" "I am the *way*." And that way is the link that connects the home from which we set out with the place we are going to. So with Jesus. He is "the way." Every step you tread, from the very first till you reach the city, is Jesus—"Jesus only." If there be not a way, then you can never reach your destination. If you be not in Jesus, the true "way," how can you ever reach the city of God?

But more. When you are on the way, you want above all things to be sure that it is the *right* one. You are a stranger. You look anxiously round for a finger-post or for some traveler to tell you it is the *true* way you are walking in. Thus we have the next point—"the *truth*." Jesus is the "*way*." Jesus is the "*true*" way. Go on, traveler, thus, and you will be sure to reach the Father's dwelling.

But more. You are a poor, needy creature. On that way your *life* must be sustained. You must have life kept up on the *way*, and life kept up when you reach your *destination*. This, too, is met next in Jesus. "I am the life." Thus, dear fellow traveler to Canaan, in Him we have, at our very *door*, all we need—a "way," a "true" and "living" way. Jesus only, our life in starting; Jesus only, our life on the way; Jesus only, our life when we reach the long-loved dwelling.

And mark: "No man cometh unto the *Father* but by me." He does not say "*God*." Ah, every man will have to stand before *God*. It is those only who go by Jesus that will reach the *Father*. It tells us we are children, related by the nearest and dearest of ties. It tells us of a *home* far beyond, and a *family*, and a *rich table*, and all the endearments of the heart. You may take *your own* way, if you like, and the end will be that you will reach God—but it will be a God out of Christ. It will be *God* without the *Father*. It will be judgment and terror, and justice and wrath. If you want to see the *Father*, either now or hereafter, you must come by Jesus. He is the only way laid down by Heaven, but laid down at your very door.

Yet, ignorant and slow as the disciples were, there is only one thing that will "suffice." "Lord, show us the Father, and it sufficeth us." He is the only One that can meet man's heart. He is a stranger in the wilderness. He has no home—no loving hand to lead him on. The cry of his heart is, "I want a Father." Jesus is that Father. In Him the wilderness ends. In Him the table is spread. The heart rests. Its joy is full. It is "sufficed."

"He that hath seen *me* hath seen the Father;" "believe me that I am in the Father, and the Father in me." These words contain a deep truth on which the intellect of the day would do well to meditate. If you wanted to see the *whole world*, and some one presented you with a map, you would have on that map all that you needed. If you were taken and shown that world, you would see nothing more than what you had seen on the map. The difference would be, not in the *reality* of the thing, but in the *expansion* of the reality. Or if you wanted to see all the glorious objects that hang over our heads on a starry night, and some one gave you a sketch of them exactly as they are, you would need no more, even though some hand might lead you to each planet. When you had seen all, you would but have seen the sketch *expanded*. To the *reality* your soaring could add nothing.

Just so is Jesus to us. He is as the sketch, the plan, the pattern of the reality. "No man hath *seen God at any time;* the only begotten Son, in the bosom of the Father, *He hath declared Him.*" "He that hath seen *me* hath seen the *Father.*" He is the great *Unseen,* condensed as it were. He is the Invisible, *accommodated* to man's vision, to man's grasp. If it were even possible to see *God,* you could see nothing more than you see in Jesus. After your loftiest attainments, you have seen only an *expansion.*

Jesus is the point of contact between the Infinite Jehovah on one side, and finite man on the other. Man cannot sound the depths of *space* and *eternity* to see God. And yet he must see Him. How? If the thing is to be accomplished, it must be by the Infinite meeting man. So God came within man's grasp by taking a *body.* Now man can grasp God—the Infinite, Invisible, Unsearchable Jehovah—in the person of the Lord Jesus. What a blessing for the ever-soaring intellect! What a resting-place when, after struggling and striving, it returns baffled from the endeavor—the *vain* endeavor – to grasp the *Infinite!* What a resting-place at the feet of Jesus—there, without the stretching of the faculties or the groping of the intellect to look into the face of Jesus and see the *face,* the *look,* the *smile* of God!

Mark another thought connected with this, poor searcher after God! Suppose it were possible for thee to grasp the Infinite. Yet that which the mind is able to comprehend comes in course of time to lose its power over it. It becomes a tame thing. The mind soars on to something *beyond.* How then is this yearning of man's immortal soul to be met? The mind must have a God that it can *com-*

prehend, and yet He must be of such a nature as to be *incomprehensible*—One that, no matter how much the mind can *grasp*, it will always find *behind* something it has not reached. To this question no answer could ever have been given had not Jesus come. The mind can grasp Him, and yet there is *God* in Him, so that, let man soar as high as he may, there is always that behind which no mind has ever reached, or can reach. "He that has seen *me* hath seen the *Father*." What a sweet resting-place for the lofty intellect of man! Oh how beautiful does intellect appear when seen reposing at the feet of Jesus! Yes, *He* is the point of contact between the finite and the Infinite, between God and man; with "all the fullness" of the infinite God treasured up in Him on the one hand, and the perfect nature of man on the other, sin only excepted.

And observe the spiritual significance of our Lord's following words, "Verily, verily, I say unto you, He that believeth on me, the works that I do shall he do also; and greater works than these shall he do." Our power of working effectually for God is not believing in *ourselves*, but in the heart being fixed on Jesus—"He that believeth on *me*." Yes, there is the secret of great works. There is the source of all spiritual success. The more whole-hearted you are for Christ, the more will you work, and work effectually. You can do with this what you could not do with all your self-reliance or qualifications and endowments. O Christian reader, forget it not! Let nothing come between your heart and the Saviour, for then you will "sow much, but bring in little; you will eat, but you will not have enough; you will drink, but you will not be *filled* with drink; you will clothe you, but not be warm; you will earn wages, but only to put it into a bag with holes."

And observe the two closing verses of this portion of God's word. "At that day ye shall know that I am in my Father, and *ye in me*, and *I in you*. He that hath my commandments, and keepeth them, he it is that loveth me; and he that loveth me shall be loved of my Father, and I will love him, and will manifest myself to him." Mark the effect of the Spirit's descent. They were to be conscious of a *new union*. Jesus had been with them before, and *they* with Him. *Now* they should see that *He* was in them and *they* in Him. Precious bond! Holy and indissoluble connection! And this is the standing of every child of God now. He is "in Christ" *before God;* and whatever Christ is, he is also: and Christ is "in him" *down here*—his life, his joy, his all.

But how is the sweet assurance of this to be experienced by the soul? Mark the connection between it and what follows. "He that *hath* my commandments, and *keepeth* them, he it is that loveth me." It is by holiness of life. It is by having the words of the Lord Jesus in us, and the heart and conscience brought under their power. It is thus we shall realize joy and peace. Thus shall we *prove* our love to the Saviour. Thus shall we know that we are "loved of the Father." Thus will the Lord Jesus "manifest Himself" to us, and we shall feel that religion is a deep, a true reality. Thus only shall we know that which *not many know in these days*, the fullness of joy, the calmness of peace, and the victory over the world, from our souls being the dwelling-place of the Father and the Son. O reader, keep Christ's commandments! Walk in the light! Be satisfied with no *present* attainment. Press on more earnestly. Cling more than ever to Jesus. Aim higher each day. Seek the peace and joy of true religion

—not from brethren, not from doctrines or creeds, but from close personal communion with Jesus Himself. Go to the fountain. Go daily. Every other source is but a broken cistern. O keep near Jesus! Have done forever with all else but Jesus. Have a whole heart, a full heart, a loving heart, a ready heart for Jesus, "in season and out of season." So God will bless you; and thus—*only thus*—will you be a happy Christian, and a living witness for Christ.

> I have not looked upon that rainbow-girded throne,
>   Where Thou, my Saviour, sittest;
> I have not seen Thy robe of light, Thy dazzling crown,
>   Eternal King of glory!
> I have not been where tens of thousands stand
>   To minister before Thee;
> I have not entered yet that beauteous far-off land,
>   Or trod Thy Father's mansions;
>   'Tis true—I have not seen Thee,
>   And yet I think I love Thee.
>
> I have not seen Thee walking on this dark, sad earth,
>   A way-worn Man of sorrow,
> With bitter shame and grief acquainted from Thy birth,
>   A King, despised, rejected;
> I cannot call to mind Thy thorn-encircled brow,
>   Bedewed with drops of anguish;
> I have not traced the print of wounds, still bleeding now,
>   With rude and daring finger:
>   But though I have not seen Thee,
>   Thy grace has made me love The
>
> I have not seen Thee yet as David's holy Son,
>   With all Thy saints appearing,
> To make earth's kingdoms—long, alas! usurped—Thine own,
>   To rule and reign forever;
> But faith expects to see the glorious vision still,
>   And waits with eager longing.
> My Saviour, hasten: come; Thy precious word fulfill:
>   Oh! give Thy *promised* blessing
>   To those who have not seen Thee,
>   And yet, believing, love Thee.

THE COMING OF CHRIST.

Psalm 1, 3—6.

> Our God shall come, and shall not keep silence: a fire shall devour before him, and it shall be very tempestuous round about him. He shall call to the heavens from above, and to the earth, that he may judge his people. Gather my saints together unto me; those that have made a covenant with me by sacrifice. And the heavens shall declare his righteousness: for God *is* judge himself. Selah.

WE stand on the eve of one of the greatest events the world has ever witnessed. Signs are multiplying on every side of us, compared with which there has been no parallel either in the history of the Church or the world. One of the greatest changes to both hangs upon this great event. It is the coming of the Lord Jesus Christ the second time, in power and glory, to bring all things in subjection to Himself, and to be "King of kings and Lord of lords." Let us see what the psalmist says of this event in the passage under consideration.

The first word is a striking one—"*Our* God." It is the *family* word. None but the child can use it. That child is one of the family. He is related to his heavenly Father. He has been redeemed and brought nigh by the blood of Christ. He is in the bonds of the everlasting covenant. He is a joint-heir with Christ. He can look up and say,

"My beloved is mine, and I am His." He will be able to say with joy, when the Lord shall descend from heaven in flaming fire, "Lo, this is *our* God; we have waited for Him, and He will save us: this is the Lord; we have waited for Him; we will be glad and rejoice in His salvation." Yes, it is the family word. He who now puts into our lips the sweet word, "Our Father," enables us to look forward to that solemn hour, and say, "*Our* God."

We are about to meditate on a solemn scene — God coming down to this earth in a human form as a devouring fire, with storms and tempests raging around Him. Oh, how necessary to be able to say, before we gaze upon it, "*Our* God!" What will it be if we cannot say, "*Our* God"? With what feelings of terror and alarm must it be viewed, unless we can say in prospect, "*Our* God"! Make sure of this, reader, before you go one step farther. Only this can make you calm in the prospect, and in the reality, when it comes, to be able to say, "*Our* God." Therefore it is that the Holy Spirit puts this little word first, on which we may dwell earnestly, solemnly, searchingly, before we proceed to that which follows.

"Our God shall come, and shall not keep silence." In order clearly to understand what is meant here by God "not keeping silence," we must refer to the closing part of the chapter, from the sixteenth verse to the twenty-second. "But unto the wicked God saith, What hast thou to do to declare my statutes, or that thou shouldest take my covenant in thy mouth? Seeing thou hatest instruction, and castest my words behind thee. When thou sawest a thief, then thou consentedst with him, and hast been partaker with adulterers. Thou givest thy mouth to evil, and thy tongue frameth deceit. Thou sittest and speakest against thy brother; thou slanderest thine own mother's son. These things hast thou done, and *I kept silence;* thou thoughtest that I was *altogether such an one as thyself.*" Here God reviews the character of the wicked in this dispensation. It is exactly what has been going on in our world for the last six thousand years. Men have been taking God's covenant "*in their mouth;*" in other words, making a *profession* of religion, while all the time the *power* of religion has been absent. Underneath this profession, sin and iniquity of the worst form has been carried on. Men have really been "hating" God, and "casting His words behind them." "Theft," "adultery," "evil," "deceit," "false witness," "slander"—have not all these things been going on in the world at a fearful speed? All this while God has "kept silence." He has not interfered to strike men down in such acts with His arm of judgment; so they begin to say, "'Where is God?' Tush! 'doth God see?' If there be a God, why does He not interfere? Either there is none, or else He is 'altogether such an one as ourselves.'" Thus the world has gone on —the wicked "flourishing as a green bay tree," the righteous returning with a "full cup" of tears, and God keeping silence. But it shall not always be so. "Our God shall come, and *shall not keep silence.*" He shall come and "reprove" man, and "set" each act and deed "in order" "before the eyes" of the wicked. It is interesting to notice how nearly all the features of the wicked, described in this chapter, and which history has endorsed as the dominant principles in the world, are again reproduced by the Holy Spirit in the third chapter of St. Paul's Second Epistle to Timothy, and which are to be more prominently developed—as the flower from the bud—in the last days.

And what are to be the heralds of the Lord's coming? "A fire shall devour before Him, and it shall be very tempestuous round about him." Here again the Holy Spirit confirms this testimony by St. Paul: "And to you who are troubled rest with us, when the Lord Jesus shall be revealed from heaven with His mighty angels, in flaming fire taking vengeance on them that know not God, and that obey not the gospel of our Lord Jesus Christ: who shall be punished with everlasting destruction from the presence of the Lord, and from the glory of His power." Yes, from one end of Christendom to the other, one piercing cry shall rend the heavens: "Ye rocks and hills, fall upon us, and hide us from the presence of the Lamb." The entreaty, earnest and loud, will then be heard from many a lip that now scorns the preaching of the Cross: "Lord, Lord, open to us." But "too late." Why should men clamor as to the question of hell, whether or not it will be material fire? Memory will play a conspicuous part in that day. The recollection of grace so freely offered, but vilely spurned, and this for a lifetime, will make man's existence a hell, compared with which the torment of material fire and brimstone will be as nothing. It shall be "*very* tempestuous." The nations shall be at their wits' end. The ties of nature and of society shall be set at nought. Men's lusts and passions shall have unbridled course. They shall run to and fro. Knowledge shall increase. Men's hearts on all sides will be "failing them for fear, looking after those things that are coming on the earth." A few will lift up their heads, in that universal wreck and ruin, calmly and joyfully; for *they* know their redemption is nigh, their hour of triumph at hand. Oh, to stand among that little band in that awful hour, and be able to say, "*Our* God"!

But what will the Lord do then? "He shall call to the heavens from above, and to the earth, that He may judge His people." He shall call to the *heavens*—to the spirits of the departed ones—those who have lived and died in the Lord, and are now with Jesus; "and to the earth"—to the bodies now in dust, that the spirits may again inhabit them. Not only so; He shall call to the *earth*—to the saints of the Lord then alive and remaining. The loved ones who have left us, and those who remain, shall be called by His voice. Again the Spirit of God confirms this testimony by St. Paul: "For this we say unto you by the word of the Lord, that we which are alive and remain unto the coming of the Lord shall not prevent them which are asleep. For the Lord Himself shall descend from heaven with a shout, with the voice of the archangel, and with the trump of God: and the *dead in Christ* shall rise *first: then* we which are *alive and remain* shall be caught up together with them in the clouds, to meet the Lord in the air: and so shall we ever be with the Lord." The word rendered "then" (επειτα) in this passage, may be more correctly rendered "after that," and shows us that some interval may elapse between the meeting of the dead saints and the living ones before they are taken up to meet the Lord in the air. At some solemn and unexpected moment, when perhaps we may be in the railway carriage, in the street, in the house, or at the counter, we shall suddenly become the subjects of an instantaneous and mysterious change; and at the same moment we shall find at our very sides those whom we loved on earth, but from whom death had parted us. There shall be an interval. The fond greeting, the loved embrace, the outburst of joy shall fill it up. Then all shall rise together at one and the same summons from on high, "and so shall we ever be with the Lord." "Ever with the Lord!" Oh, the joy of those words! Here thought fails; the lips falter; the mind shrinks. Eternity alone can tell their depth. We wait to sound their meaning. Who would not say, in such a world of sin, and sorrow, and death, as this, "Come, Lord Jesus, come quickly?"

But mark the psalmist's words. Who are they that are called? "Gather my saints together unto me." What an expressive word—"My saints"! How the Lord appropriates them as His own! "They shall be mine, in that day when I make up my jewels." What precious words —"my saints," "my jewels"! What sinful, erring creatures we are! How do we daily and hourly provoke the Lord who loves us! What naughty children the Lord has to manage! How He may say of us as Moses said of Israel, "Ye have been rebellious against the Lord since the day that I knew you"! and yet, "my saints!" "my jewels!" Oh, what grace! what wondrous love!

Mark another word here. "*Gather* my saints." "He shall gather the lambs in His arms." He shall "gather" them as a shepherd his sheep in the hour of weakness and danger—the weak ones, the nervous ones, those who start at a shadow and tremble at the fluttering of a leaf. They shall not be weak or nervous then. The frail body shall be dropped forever, and they shall be clasped in an embrace such as they have never known on earth, to a bosom of infinite love.

But observe the next word. "Gather my saints *together*." It is the family meeting; it is the grand re-union; it is the glad *assembly*. We shall not rise to meet the Lord individually—in isolations; we shall be gathered *to-*

gether. So the apostle speaks of our "gathering together unto Him." And again, "We which are alive and remain shall be caught up *together with them.*" No more separations; no more divisions; no more discords; no more sects or systems: all together! One mind, one heart, one joy, one glad meeting, without the shadow of a farewell ever darkening its shores! What heart does not bound at the thought?

And yet one word more—the sweetest of all—"unto *me.*" Ah! what would all the others be without this? Nothing, nothing! The foam, the dust, the shadow, the air! What would *that* meeting be without Jesus? What is *any* meeting without Him? The very notes of heaven would be discord. Its jasper walls would be hideous. Its very air would be oppressive. It would all be dreariness, and darkness, and death. With His name every song is sweet. In His smile every countenance is bright. Every chord of the golden harps will vibrate with His praise. Every voice will be vocal with His name. Jesus, Jesus, Jesus!—throughout eternity. For this the Lord Himself prays: "Father, I will that they also whom Thou hast given me be with me *where I am*, that they may behold my glory." Love can only be satisfied with the presence of its object. So with the Saviour. He longs for us. He waits for us. We *must* be with Him. How can He be happy without us?

But who are those thus gathered? Mark it well, reader: "Those that have made a covenant with me by sacrifice." They are those who have made a covenant with God through the sacrifice of the Lord Jesus Christ. They are the *blood-* bought ones. They are those who have cast themselves —all sin and guilt, helpless and undone—on the finished work of the Lord Jesus. They are those who cry from the depths of their hearts—

> "Other refuge have I none:
> Hangs my helpless soul on Thee."

Reader, have you done this? If you have not, you are not in the covenant; and if you are not in that covenant now, can you think of *that* meeting? You may hide this sad picture from your conscience, or, worse than all, charge your sin on God by a series of excuses. But it will not avail then. Mark the next verse: "The heavens shall declare His righteousness; for God is judge Himself." His righteous dealings will then be acknowledged by every lip, and felt by every heart. Even the wicked shall be compelled to own it. And not only so, but righteousness shall be written on everything, as it never has been yet. And why? "For God is judge Himself." He shall be judge in the earth, and the result will be righteous judgment. Misrule, injustice, oppression, will all end then. "Righteousness shall cover the earth, as the waters cover the sea."

And what is the practical lesson from all this, for the world as well as God's people? There is a word for each at the close of this chapter. "Ye that forget God, consider this." Unconverted reader, weigh it well, lest God "tear thee in pieces." The day is at hand. Consider. Flee to Jesus. He is your only hope. Out of Him you are not safe for a moment. Be warned, and haste to the refuge.

Christian, "order your conversation"—or citizenship—"aright." Aim to glorify Jesus. Let His praise fill your heart. Let His image be clearly written on every act of your life. Be *whole-hearted* for Christ.

"To him that overcometh will I grant to sit with me in my throne, even as I also overcame, and am set down with my Father in His throne. He that hath an ear, let him hear, what the Spirit saith unto the churches."

> Not here, not here; not where the sparkling waters
>   Fade into mocking sands as we draw near,
> Where in the wilderness each footstep falters;
>   "I shall be satisfied," but oh! not here.
>
> Not here, where all the dreams of bliss deceive us,
>   Where the worn spirit never gains its goal;
> Where, haunted ever by the thoughts that grieve us,
>   Across us floods of bitter memory roll.
>
> There is a land where every pulse is thrilling
>   With rapture earth's sojourners may not know;
> Where heaven's repose the weary heart is stilling,
>   And peacefully life's time-tossed currents flow.
>
> Far out of sight, while sorrow still enfolds us,
>   Lies the fair country where our hearts abide
> And of its bliss is nought more wondrous told us,
>   Than these few words—"I shall be satisfied."
>
> "I shall be satisfied:" the spirit's yearning
>   For sweet companionship with kindred minds;
> The silent love that here meets no returning,
>   The inspiration which no language finds.
>
> Shall they be satisfied—the soul's vain longing,
>   The aching void which nothing earthly fills?
> Oh what desires upon my heart are thronging,
>   As I look upward to the heavenly hills!
>
> Thither my weak and weary steps are tending:
>   Saviour and Lord with Thy frail child abide;
> Guide me towards home, where, all my wanderings ended,
>   I shall see Thee, and "shall be satisfied."

THE COMMUNION OF SAINTS.

Malachi iii, 16.

Then they that feared the Lord spake often one to another: and the Lord hearkened, and heard it: and a book of remembrance was written before him for them that feared the Lord, and that thought upon his name.

We see in these words the existence of a spirit of union bringing those of kindred sympathies into closer intercourse while they were passing through the sorrows they had to endure. They that feared the Lord were evidently a very small remnant in the nation; they were its salt, and had not lost their savor, yet they were not sufficient for its preservation. In the 9th verse we have this declaration, " Ye are cursed with a curse, for ye have robbed me, even this whole nation." The tithes were not brought into the temple; those that worked wickedness were set up, and the proud were called happy. The righteous were as a lamp despised; the ways of Zion mourned; none came to her solemn feasts, and astonishment possessed those that feared the Lord. Things are not very different in our day, and we see, as the Psalmist did, the wicked spreading himself as a green bay tree, provoking our envy, and exciting our discontent, unless we are brought to understand his end; for of the wicked God has said, "He shall receive of the fruit of his doings, and it shall go ill with him." These or similar causes still exist to bring into closer union those who fear the Lord as a source of mutual comfort and support. As, therefore, we see that such communings are hearkened to and approved by the Lord, and such gracious promises are made to those who fear Him, we may well inquire what are their distinguishing features, that we may see if we have any well-grounded evidence of being of the number. We therefore notice—

1st. What it is to fear the Lord.

2d. Of what they spoke.

3d. That this communion of the saints is pleasing to the Lord.

4th. The gracious declaration God has made concerning them.

1st. I have heard the application of these words to many who had, in truth, small pretensions to the character; timidity of disposition, morality, and natural meekness of spirit being miscalled godly fear. Fear is either natural, slavish, or filial. The first is common to animal as well as to rational creatures, disposing them to avoid danger or evils, either real or imaginary. Slavish fear is seen in the mariners of the ship in which Jonah was a passenger, and in Felix, under Paul's preaching; also in the people brought from Babylon, of whom it is said, in 2 Kings xvii, 32, "So they feared the Lord, and made unto themselves, of the lowest of them, priests of the high places." Filial fear is distinct from both these, and is that holy habit of reverence for God, wrought in the heart by the Holy Ghost, as a spirit of adoption, by which the soul is brought to trust in Him, and to have strong confidence in His faithfulness.

It is a grace of great activity, and is called a fountain of life; it is a pure and holy principle, and teaches men to depart from iniquity and to hate evil. It is said of Christ that He shall be of a "quick understanding in the fear of the Lord." It may be said to be a principle that teaches us respect for that which is good, from a pure love to it. Its motives are of the highest order, and as the vicegerent of the Holy Ghost, is the light within us. It instructs the conscience, and enables it to arrive at just conclusions, and such as are in harmony with the will of God as revealed in His word. It may be forced, but it cannot be silenced, and blessed is the man who at all times gives heed to its faithful monitions. It is no flatterer, but, according to its power, asserts the authority of God in the soul, and bears testimony to the purity of the truth; so that its record on the heart is a testimony both to God's holiness and man's corruption. It is not guided by the traditions, nor taught by the precepts of men, but by the word of God. God's testimonies are the delight of the soul that fears Him, and by His grace it adheres to them. His statutes are its song in the house of its pilgrimage, and when His words are found they are the joy and the rejoicing of the heart. The fear of the Lord, therefore, incites to good and preserves from evil, and delivers from pride, arrogance, and every false way. It makes its possessor tremble at God's word, lest he fall into the evils and errors it condemns, and teaches us to choose affliction rather than iniquity.

2d. We inquire what those who feared the Lord spoke about. They were certainly not a speculative society, nor one without cohesion and sympathy, otherwise their communications would have been less frequent; "but they spake often one to another." Doubtless they spoke of themselves, and of what they once were; this is a common topic with God's people. They have a deep sense of their sinfulness, and of the greatness of the divine mercy, as exhibited in their salvation. This consciousness of the Lord's unmerited favor exercises a great influence on them, and they are found expressing it frequently, and in a variety of ways, in these holy songs, as well as in their friendly communings. They speak of the wondrousness of that divine sovereignty that, as an act of grace, plucked them as brands from the burning. Their admiration of the entire plan of salvation, as devised by infinite wisdom, is a constant theme with them, while they lament the narrowness of their views, the shallowness of their thoughts, conceptions, and feelings on this vast, deep, grand and glorious subject. Thus, confession of their great ignorance not unfrequently occupies their time. When walking in the light and comfort of the healing beams of the Sun of Righteousness, they delight to speak of special tokens of the Lord's love, the sweetness of the promises, and the blessedness their souls enjoy when His delivering power is felt in the soul. But they also know and speak of the watchman's cry, "The morning cometh and also the night." They have their changes, that fear God, and while at times they shout from the tops of the mountains, at others, feeling a horror of great darkness come upon them, they fear to call Him theirs. These gloomy doubts are not unfrequently discussed by them, and the burden of their song has been aptly expressed by Dr. Watts:—

> "Oh! could we make those doubts remove,
> Those gloomy doubts that rise,
> And view the Canaan that we love
> With unbeclouded eyes."

And, in the words of Newton, we get another clue to the thread of their discourse :—

> "I often hear Thy children talk,
>   And I believe 'tis even true,
> How with delight Thy ways they walk,
>   And gladly thy commandments do.
>
> "I look into my heart, and read
>   Accounts so very diff'rent there,
> That had I not Thy blood to plead,
>   The sight would drive me to despair."

But, to abbreviate these remarks, they talk of His second coming without sin unto salvation; of the gospel's glorious sound reaching from pole to pole; to that time when Egypt will be the third with God, and Ethiopia spread abroad her hands and worship. They sometimes talk of the consummation of all things, the last judgment, and the everlasting happiness of all His saints. But, while they thus talk, they want a present, divine assurance that the wonders which eye hath not seen, nor ear heard, shall be beheld by them, and that, when He shall stand upon the earth in the latter days, they shall see Him for themselves, and not for another.

3d. Their talking to one another is pleasing to God. What wondrous words must they have uttered that Deity should hearken with approval! with such approval that, lest the subject matter of their converse should pass into oblivion, "a book of remembrance was written" of it before Him; not to refresh the memory of Omniscience, but for "them that feared the Lord, and that thought upon His name." What is this "book of remembrance," if not the Bible? In it are recorded the sorrows and joys, the darkness and light, the bondage and liberty, the confusion and peace, the condemnation and justification, the present troubles and future felicity of His people. In it are the songs of David, the sighings of Jeremiah, and the psalms of Asaph. Its exordium is rendered sad by the murder of Abel, and its peroration jubilant by the glorious invitation to "whosoever will," to "take the water of life freely." Herein are accounts of wilderness trials and Jehovah-Jireh deliverances. Herein is the dialogue of those two who walked by the way and were sad, while as yet He who joined them on the road was unknown to them. This, then, is the book written for them that fear the Lord, and for those who think upon His name. This communion of saints is well-pleasing to God, who has exhorted us "to do good and communicate forget not, for with such sacrifices God is well pleased."

4th and lastly. The promise God has made: "They shall be mine, saith the Lord, in the day that I make up my jewels, and I will spare them as a man spareth his own son that serveth him." The opposite of this shall be the lot of the wicked; "reprobate silver shall men call them, because the Lord hath rejected them." See, then, the doctrine of our text; our interchange of spiritual experience, whether the narrative of sorrow or joy, is well-pleasing to God, while it is our comfort in the land of our affliction. But the time will come when sighing and sorrowing shall flee away, when we shall repose beside everlasting fountains of living water, solaced by the fruit of the tree of life, and raised to an ecstasy of delight by melodious sounds borne on aromatic breezes. Then we shall be entranced by the splendor, glory, and bliss of the beatific vision of God and the Lamb, forever and ever.

W. Hunt.

www.ingramcontent.com/pod-product-compliance
Lightning Source LLC
Chambersburg PA
CBHW020902230426
43666CB00008B/1282